Haynes

The first **40** years | 1960 to the new millennium

The very beginning. John Haynes with his 1954 Austin Seven Special, taken with a Brownie box camera.

Haynes

The first **40** years   1960 to the new millennium

Jeff Clew

Haynes Publishing

Dedication

To my dear wife Annette for all her good advice, hard work and encouragement over the years, and also to all those members of staff, past and present, who have helped to secure the success and growth of the Group.

John H. Haynes

First edition published 1985 as *Haynes: The First 25 Years*
This edition published 2000

A catalogue record for this book is available from the British Library

ISBN 1 85960 418 8

Library of Congress catalog card no. 99-80189

Published by Haynes Publishing, Sparkford, Nr Yeovil, Somerset BA22 7JJ, England.

Tel. 01963 442030 Fax 01963 440001
Int. tel. +44 1963 442030 Fax +44 1963 440001
E-mail: sales@haynes-manuals.co.uk
Web site: www.haynes.co.uk

Haynes North America, Inc.,
861 Lawrence Drive, Newbury Park,
California 91320, USA

Printed and bound in England by
J. H. Haynes & Co. Ltd, Sparkford

Contents

Foreword

I have a confession to make. I love cars and feel very lucky to have been able to spend most of my working life publishing books about them and, of course, motorcycles too. It was a real pleasure to work on the first edition of this company history published in 1985 with Jeff Clew, the author, and Jane Marshall, the editor.

Then as now, with the publication of the second edition timed suitably enough to celebrate the new millennium, this book has brought me back into contact with what publishing is all about, and that is the creation of a manuscript, the editorial directing of it by Darryl Reach, the picture selection, and so on – all totally removed from the constant making of business decisions which inevitably, as the company has grown, has become part of my day-to-day activity. It has also of course, been a trip of pure nostalgia, recalling to mind people and events from long ago.

Every schoolboy has his heroes, and I was no exception, one of mine being William Morris. I still have the book *Wheels to Fortune* by James Leasor (presented to me on 1 July 1955 for the Senior Art Prize by my headmaster at Sutton Valence School, near Maidstone, Kent), and I would like to quote from it:

> For any man worth his salt, the desire for personal gain is not his chief reason for working. It is a desire to achieve, to be a success, to make his job worthy of his mettle and self-respect.
> Money plays an important part in this – it is stupid to deny it – but it is the part of the air to living things . . .
>
> *Lord Nuffield as W. R. Morris, 1927*

The way the company has grown over the years is a source of continuing amazement to me. Much of its growth and success must be attributed to the loyalty, dedication and enthusiasm of the company's worldwide employees and I would like to thank them and think that this appreciation of their efforts is reflected throughout the book.

John Haynes OBE with the beautiful 7-litre straight-eight, twin overhead camshaft 1931 Model J Duesenberg Derham Tourster; the only one in Europe.

John H. Haynes, OBE
1 January 2000

About the author

Jeff Clew joined J. H. Haynes & Co Ltd during November 1972 to start up the range of Haynes *Motorcycle Owners Workshop Manuals*. As a result, he wrote the first ten in ten months before recruiting additional authors to help build up the list. When G. T. Foulis was acquired in 1973 he also became involved with the motorcycle titles bearing this imprint, again originating some of them himself working from home in a freelance capacity. As Haynes's motorcycle publishing grew, he grew with it, to become Managing Editor in February 1978 and Editorial Director by the end of that year. Shortly after this appointment he also became a Director of G. T. Foulis, and later still, the Executive Editorial Director of the Haynes Publishing Group. He retired in February 1991, by which time he had written 19 manuals and 18 books.

An enthusiastic motorcyclist since 1946, Jeff has ridden in a wide range of competition events, and even dabbled with speedway. He still rides today, mostly in events organised by the Vintage MCC, using one or other of his small collection of machines. He is married and now that both his daughters have left home he and his wife have returned to the village of Queen Camel. It was there that the family first lived after moving west in 1973 soon after he had joined Haynes.

Jeff Clew, the author (seated) with John Haynes, left and Darryl Reach, Editorial Director of the Special Interest Publishing Division, on the occasion of the launch of *Sparkford: Memories of the Past*, 19 February 1997. *(Peter Nicholson)*

Employees and associates, past and present

Haynes employees, as at 4 January 2000

Europe

First name	Surname	First name	Surname	First name	Surname
Jonathan	Abbott	Christine	Callcott	Etienne	Gerber
Christine	Adamson	Maureen	Carr	Terry	Gibbs
Kevin	Addicott	Scott	Carson	Colin	Goodland
Monica	Andersson	Steven	Carter	Robert	Gosney
Michael	Anson	Stephen	Carver	Jillian	Gough
Joyce	Antell	Claire	Ceresa	Terrance	Grealey
Nicholas	Apsey	Jeremy	Churchill	Mark	Haim
John	Austin	Michael	Churchill	Steven	Haines
Daniel	Bacon	Stephen	Churchill	James	Harper
Joanne	Bailey	Elizabeth	Clarke	Wendy	Harris
Judith	Bailey	Ann	Cockerell	Lesley	Harrison
Marian	Banfield	Philip	Collins	Philippe	Haussin
Ian	Barnes	Graham	Cook	Annette	Haynes
Marion	Baxandall	Mark	Coombs	David	Haynes
Sara	Belton	Sharon	Cooper	John	Haynes
Barry	Benjafield	Panton	Corbett	Andrew	Hayward
Rebecca	Berridge	Tricia	Coulson	Roger	Healing
Timothy	Birch	Corrinne	Cox	Kevin	Heals
Allan	Bishop	Penelope	Cox	David	Hermelin
Kenneth	Blair	Isabelle	Creton	Simon	Hewitt
Barbara	Blake	Lee	Crompton	Jennifer	Higgins
Darren	Blower	Trudi	David	Christopher	Hill
Stephen	Bolt	Colin	Davies	Carol	Holliday
Cyrille	Bombillon	Dawn	Davies	David	House
Tracey	Bonds	Norman	Denton	Allanagh	Hubbart
Nicholas	Bown	Glyn	Dexter	Mark	Hughes
Edward	Brine	Lynn	Dickson	Mark	Hunt
Mark	Broadley	Spencer	Drayton	Derek	Hyslop
Alexandra	Brookes	Sarah	Dunlop	Krister	Ingvarsson
Louisa	Brown	Mark	Eddleston	Emma	Isaacs
Peter	Bryant	Nicholas	Ewers	Nelson	James
Paul	Buckland	Vivienne	Fillery	Maureen	Jasper
James	Bunkum	Keith	Fullman	Peter	Jennings

First name	Surname	First name	Surname	First name	Surname
Robert	Jex	Paul	Murphy	Shirley	Smith
Steven	John	Judith	Murray	Matthew	Sparkes
Andrew	Jones	Flora	Myer	Alan	Sperring
Tony	Kemp	Kevin	Newport	David	Suter
Anders	Kind	David	Notley	Paul	Sweby
Mandy	Kuhn	Robert	Parker	Paul	Tanswell
Janice	Lansley	Tamatha	Parker	Stephen	Tanswell
Simon	Larkin	Cassandra	Paull	Nigel	Tate
Peter	Lawrence	Max	Pearce	Anita	Taylor
Hervé	Le Bourdais	Kevin	Perrett	Viktoria	Tischer
Andrew	Legg	Victoria	Pett	Andrew	Toop
Laetitia	Lethimonnier	Jeremy	Phillips	Peter	Trott
Håkan	Lindberg	Cecilia	Rahm	Carole	Turk
Georgina	Loder	Martynn	Randall	Peter	Turner
Barbara	Lumb	Darryl	Reach	Amanda	Warry
Sandra	MacKinnon	Stephen	Rendle	John	Warry
George	Magnus	David	Richards	Kirsty	Waterton
Matthew	Marke	Jacqueline	Roberts	Michael	Webb
John	Martin	James	Robertson	Martyn	White
Pierre	Martin	Alison	Roelich	Susan	White
Richard	Martin	Peter	Rowden	David	Wilcox
Ian	Mauger	Gillian	Royal	Kim	Williams
Julian	McGeoch	Michael	Saxton	Maureen	Wincott
Louise	McIntyre	Heather	Scott	Julie	Winzar
John	Mead	Charles	Seaton	Colin	Wood
Jayne	Millett	Pascal	Sgouridis	Amal	Woodard-Eltarzi
Matthew	Minter	Peter	Shoemark	Rosemary	Yates
Denis	Morgan	Moreen	Siewcharran	Jason	Youé
Maurice	Murphy	Christine	Smith	Ronald	Young

North America and Australia

First name	Surname	First name	Surname	First name	Surname
Alan D.	Ahlstrand	Alan W.	Chatwood	Casandra L.	Henry
Jennifer J.	Albers	Angela R.	Cheatham	Brian P.	Hilderbrand
Micah A.	Allison	Nigel J.	Clements	Jess W.	Holt
Kristina L.	Anderson	Steven H.	Dykes	Wesley L.	Humphrey
Marvin E.	Anderson	Larry	Elder	Randy D.	Jackson
Barbara E.	Arden	Katherine L.	Faria	Erik J.	Johnson
Carl	Armstrong	Jill Marie	Fennel	Bonita R.	Keating
Lisa M.	Baltrushes	Mickee A.	Ferrell	Jeffrey L.	Kibler
Emmett Lee	Barrett	Eileen M.	Fore	Jeff B.	Killingsworth
Carey A. T.	Bates	Michael L.	Forsythe	Mark A.	Kinsey
Darrell G.	Belvin	Joseph R.	Gaines	Ryan J.	Koss
Daniel M.	Benhardus	James D.	Gatlin	James	Laux
Hoyte T.	Black	Kenneth J.	Gearhart	Debra A.	Layne
Heidi M.	Bly	Marcell Soliz	Gibbel	Robert P.	Maddox
William J.	Bolyard	Eric W.	Godfrey	Mark C.	Magner
Amy M.	Brewer	Gerhild E.	Harlow	Anthony A. III	Magnier
Don B.	Brown	Gregory A.	Harnack	Jay R.	Mansfield
Melissa D.	Burnett	Diana M.	Hartman	Wendy L.	Marshall
Silvia J.	Castillo	Jonathan D.	Henderson	Scott	Mauck
Victoria D.	Chapman	Robert A.	Henderson	David M.	McDonald

First name	Surname	First name	Surname	First name	Surname
Mammie E.	McGowan	Penny S.	Peters	Gordon J.	Stengel
Rogelio J.	Melgar	Rosemarie L.	Prater	David W.	Stittums
James A.	Nicholson	Clarence E.	Proctor	Jay D.	Storer
Debra A.	Norbut	Edward V.	Pulk	Michael D.	Stubblefield
Eric	Oakley	Kent H II	Reppert	Khemis L.	Thomas
Linda S.	Oates	Debra J.	Rife	Dale E.	Vandiver
Elizabeth L.	O'Neill	Rick R.	Riggins	Nicholas A.	Walsh
Mangkone	Onsourathoum	Jaime Jr.	Sarte	Bonita G.	Whittle
Charles E.	Oxsher	Jerrie D.	Scott	George R.	Winters
Lisa R.	Ozment	Rita	Simmons	Lawrence E.	Warren
Babak	Parsi	James Robert Jr	Simpson	John A.	Wegmann
Kristin M.	Patton	Lonnie R.	Singleton	Cameron	Young

Past members who made a most useful contribution while they were with the Group

Gill	Andrew	Richard	Henwood	Barry	Piggott
Hazel	Atkinson	Betty	Hill	Gary	Pippard
Joan	Bird	Rita	Hill	Les	Purcell
Peter	Bishop	Brian	Horsfall	Stanley	Randolph
Les	Brazier	Lynn	House	John	Ridgers
John	Brooks	Alan	Howden	Margaret	Robus
Jeff	Clew	Colin	Hughes	Alec	Rollo
Ian	Coomber	Rob	Iles	John	Rose
Nick	Cudmore	Mandy	Jeans	Jim	Scott
Sheila	Curtis	Helen	Logreco	Simon	Slade
Mansur	Darlington	Andy	Lynch	Tim	Snook
Terry	Davey	Jane	Marshall	Barry	Squance
Frank	Day	Ann	Mathieson	Roger	Stagg
David	de la Hey	Harold	Miller	Peter	Strasman
Ron	Encell	Terry	Mitchell	Bette	Stulle
Len	Goodland	Peggy	Nation	Annie	Toomey
Rod	Grainger	Peter	Nicholson	Ron	Tucker
Terry	Grimwood	Jan	O'Donohue	Peter	Vallis
Albert	Haines	Pete	O'Donohue	Robin	Wager
John	Hall	Tim	Parker	Peter	Ward
John H. C.	Haynes	Annette	Pearce	Chris	Wilding
Harold S.	Haynes	Mike	Pereira	Andy	Youngs

And to thank all those many others who have also played their part but are not mentioned.

Haynes Motor Museum permanent staff and regular volunteers

Maurice	Banbury	Shirley	Cox	Pauline	Penn
Andrew	Brasher	Julie	Gill	Janice	Romans
Jane	Brasher	Christopher	Haynes	Emma	Taylor
Ralph	Brasher	Marc	Haynes	Adrian	Trevorrow
David	Carlton	Stephanie	Knock		
John	Carlton	Oliver	New		
Derek	Chant	Mike	Penn		

Introduction and acknowledgements

When John Haynes asked me if I would update the original edition of this book I accepted with great pleasure, the more so as its publication would coincide with the new Millennium and the company's 40th Anniversary. I must confess I had a few inner reservations at first because the circumstances under which it would be written would be very different from those that existed in 1985. Then I was the Group's Executive Editorial Director and had access to what may be regarded as sensitive information, as well as to all my colleagues with whom I had worked since late 1972.

Thirteen years on I was into my eighth year of retirement and many to whom I would have liked to talk were no longer with the company. Most of those who had replaced them I knew only by name and I had to be quite sure I could get at all the facts I needed.

Fortunately, any fears I may have had never materialised. Everyone could not have been more helpful. Despite having a heavy workload they all managed to find time to see me. My questions were patiently answered and all the changes that had taken place in recent years were explained in detail. Even the precis I sent to them after our conversation was checked, to ensure it was factually correct and the opportunity taken to add anything that inadvertently had been overlooked. I would prefer not to mention individual names in this context as I would be listing most of the company's senior management.

Overall, compiling the update has proved to be a fascinating exercise. Having worked for the company for a shade under 19 years, and being a shareholder, it was to be expected that I would maintain a keen interest in company affairs. As my retirement more or less coincided with the depression of the early 1990s when the company was at its lowest ebb, researching the updating material gave me a detailed overview of how the recovery plan had been formulated and implemented.

Special thanks are due to John and Annette Haynes for their personal contributions, and to Peter Nicholson, with whom I worked in complete accord while he was editing the text.

Jeff Clew
Queen Camel,
December 1999

1

The birth of an idea

When, in 1967, John Haynes decided to resign his commission in the RAF so that he could devote his full time to his publishing business, his friends thought he was mad. When they heard that he would receive no pension and no gratuity, they were convinced – and secretly thought he was destined to a life of poverty. As things turned out, of course, they couldn't have been more wrong ... but let's start at the beginning.

It all started in 1954 when John Haynes was a 16-year-old schoolboy at Sutton Valence boarding school in Kent. He had decided to build himself an Austin Seven Special. At that time, Special building wasn't uncommon (except perhaps amongst 16-year-old schoolboys) because sports cars, especially the most sought after MGs, were both expensive and scarce – scarce because most of them were being exported to the States. Austin Sevens, on the other hand, could be bought quite cheaply and modified relatively easily. Having been left by a godfather a small legacy of £100 which wasn't to be touched until he was 21, John prevailed upon his parents (then living in Ceylon) to make the money available to him. They released it and with this he purchased for £15 a 750cc Austin Seven, and then all the materials needed for the conversion.

A local blacksmith flattened the springs so that the chassis could be lowered, and after raking the steering column, lowering the scuttle and rebuilding the engine, the new body was built in wood and clad with aluminium sheet. Only the original bonnet and front seats were retained, in addition to the chassis, radiator and running gear. The end result was a quite pleasing and sporty-looking car.

John got great fun out of driving it around the school playing fields for a year until his 17th birthday when the attractions of a driving licence and a car for daily road use replaced it. The reason he couldn't put his Special on the road was that it had a more or less straight-through silencer, and the only weather protection was afforded by two aero-screens. When the decision was made to sell it, a two-line advertisement in *Motor Sport* brought the amazing response of over 150 replies, which indicated the tremendous amount of interest in this grass roots activity of Special building.

Having acquired a great deal of useful, practical experience when building his 750cc Austin Seven Special, the thought occurred to John that this could be put to good use if he were to write and publish a complete set of instructions. A 48-page booklet resulted, titled *Building a 750cc Special*. It contained many line drawings because John, having just been awarded the school Senior Art Prize, was aware that drawings could be reproduced by a stencil duplicator if a stylus was used to draw on the wax stencil. A total of 250 copies of the booklet were run off, hand-folded and hand-stapled, binding tape being applied to hide the stapling on the spine. Priced at 5s (25p) per copy, the entire stock was sold in ten days during the summer of 1956, after an advertisement had been placed in *Motor Sport*. In consequence, more had to be run off which were now sold through an accommodation address in London (Modern Enterprise Distributors of 11 Old Bond Street) as conscription for National Service was imminent. Modern Enterprise Distributors was registered on 17 April 1957 as a partnership between John and his younger brother David, for the purpose of mail order trading in books. At the end of their first year's trading, a net profit of £843 16s 10d was recorded.

After completing his initial training in the RAF at their Officer Training Unit in Jurby, on the Isle of Man, John was commissioned a Pilot Officer and posted to RAF Bruggen in Germany. Whilst he was stationed there, he decided that his 750cc Specials book ought to be printed properly. Orders for it were being received in increasing numbers in London. Unable to speak German, but with the help of Marianne Vissors, a German girlfriend, he managed to find a local printer who would print his book by letterpress, setting the type in English. A thousand copies were ordered on this basis while John wrote and illustrated another, somewhat similar book, but with a greatly enlarged content – *How to Build Austin Seven Specials*. In turn this was followed by a *Ford Special Builder's Manual*, Ford Specials being the alternative to those based on the Austin, and several other titles.

Each time he came home on leave, his MGA was loaded to capacity with books (even the spare wheel was removed to make more room for books!), this being the cheapest and easiest way of getting them home. There were books in the passenger's footwell, books on the passenger's seat and books behind the seats, and with the soft-top hood up, they were in the boot as well. There was no point in having the books printed in England as English printers at that time were slow and very expensive, whereas the opposite was true in Germany. During the whole of this time, the books were being sold by a steady stream of small mail order advertisements in various motoring magazines, the return from each being analysed most carefully and compared with the cost.

When his period of National Service came to an end, John decided he would like to become a publisher in his own right, so he rented a single-roomed office at 189 Regent Street, London. It was here that he formed J. H. Haynes & Co Ltd on 18 May 1960, by which time he had four titles in print:

Building a 750cc Special	Price 5s 0d
How to Build Ford Specials	Price 8s 11d
How to Build Austin Specials	Price 8s 11d
High Speed Driving	Price 8s 11d

Soon to be added to the list was the definitive *Austin Seven Special Builder's Manual* but, by now, he was of the opinion that the motoring world might have heard too much of John Haynes, so when writing the definitive *Ford Special Builder's Manual* he used a pseudonym for the first time – G. B. Wake. His latest book was printed in Germany too, a Minivan being used for its collection. Marianne Vissors burst out laughing when she first saw this tiny vehicle, which had been bought for its considerable carrying capacity and manoeuvrability in town. She could hardly believe her eyes, for she had been used to seeing John in either his MGA or his Mark VII Jaguar, both of which were now back in the UK.

Living on his own in London whilst working long hours by himself proved a very lonely existence and eventually John decided to renew his commission in the RAF, which resulted in a posting to Church Fenton, in Yorkshire. It was here that he built a Lotus Seven from a kit and fitted it with a 997cc Ford Formula Junior engine and straight-cut Hewland five-speed dog-engagement gearbox, racing it with moderate success. At the same time, he continued to write books in his spare time, now on subjects related to engine tuning and racing at club level. They were the first books of their kind to be published on specific subjects, other 'professional' publishers coming in two or three years later with much more expensive volumes produced to a higher standard. But, at grass roots level, what the enthusiasts wanted was not just information but information that worked, and this John was able to provide through direct participation in whatever he wrote about. By now he had found a householder in Cambridge, with an empty garage, who would stock and despatch his books, the Old Bond Street premises being too small and expensive to continue with order fulfilment from there. It was here that he used the name 'The Sporting Motorists' Bookshop' for the first time. Unfortunately a severe setback occurred when the garage caught fire and some 3,000 books were destroyed – the entire stock being uninsured. It was a lesson learned the hard way.

To help recover from this setback, John bought his own Gestetner and went back to duplicating. Working often until 1 or 2am, covered in ink (Gestetner wax stencils were messy things to put on and take off the machine), and with both arms aching from turning the handle because an electrically-operated machine would have proved too expensive, he would flop exhausted into bed, to be up again by 7am to start gathering the individual sheets before he went to work. By this time (1962), his parents had returned from Ceylon, his father having retired, to settle down at 323 St Michaels Avenue, Yeovil. With a 22ft long garage adjoining his parents' house and only their small Triumph Herald to house, it proved quite easy to convert the

The Sporting Motorists'
Bookshop at the back of the
garage at 323 St Michaels
Avenue, Yeovil, in 1963.

rearmost portion of the garage into a bookshop-cum-mini warehouse, and it was to this address that the Sporting Motorists' Bookshop was transferred to be run by his father. He undertook all the day-to-day routine of opening up the mail, despatching the books, answering the queries and cashing the postal orders and cheques received. John continued writing books, arranging for their printing and publication, and also writing and placing all the mail order advertisements. By this time a change had been made from using wax stencils to printing by offset litho, after he had discovered that it was possible to type on a special paper plate that could be printed on small offset machines such as Rotaprints and Multiliths. Although it was not possible to purchase the necessary production equipment, a deal was set up in 1962 with a Mr Roper in Cirencester who had a nearly new Multilith and undertook to print the various titles, as needed. Now, not only were his own books stocked and distributed through the Sporting Motorists' Bookshop, but also those of other publishers, which helped the embryo business to expand.

In 1963 John suffered a major accident while racing his Lotus Seven at Goodwood, when he struck a bank whilst travelling backwards at about 80mph. He was thrown out of the car, which somersaulted and continued to cartwheel down the embankment, completely demolishing a Castrol sign and

Hotting up the Elva Courier. John Haynes is seen here in the process of fitting a Weber 45 DCOE carburettor, one of several engine modifications he made to improve the car's performance.

eventually becoming a total write-off. The accident almost brought his racing career to an end and left him battered and bruised for a very long period afterwards. But on the brighter side, four weeks later he married Annette, whom he had met at a friend's flat just off the King's Road in Chelsea and had been seeing regularly for just under a year. His younger brother David was Best Man and it was on the wedding morning that David was very perturbed to find John was nowhere to be seen. Fortunately he had not gone very far, only around the corner to buy, tongue in cheek, a wedding present for his bride – an IBM electric typewriter with proportional spacing!

This machine became very well travelled – Cirencester, Aden, Nairobi, Harrogate and Yeovil – as the large battered wooden packing case proves! What was special about this machine was the fact that it would produce what looked like hot-set type as each letter had the correct space allocated to it, ie an 'i' took up a third of the space of an 'm', as opposed to ordinary typewriters where the space for each letter is the same. In addition to this, it was possible to justify the right-hand margin by marking on the first typing whether spaces should be let in or out of the line concerned by reading off a scale on the machine so that both left and right margins could be set straight. This meant of course that every page had to be typeset twice and the first 13 manuals were keyed by Annette using this IBM, several of them in the heat of Aden when she worked 8–10 hours a day, eschewing many coffee parties organised by other officers' wives and similar social events, in order to get the job done.

John and Annette had first set up home in a flat in Cirencester, as by then John had been posted to RAF South Cerney. Having recovered from his racing accident, he celebrated by purchasing an Elva Courier, which he fitted with a new MGB engine modified with works-approved full race equipment, including a gas-flowed cylinder head, full race camshaft, lightweight flywheel, competition clutch and a Weber 45 DCOE carburettor. These and other modifications gave about 130bhp, and resulted in a car that proved very competitive in club racing events.

By the time the next posting came along – to RAF Khormaksar, Aden in October 1964 – John's brother David had set up his own printing company (David M. Haynes & Co Ltd) and was printing John's books on a Rotaprint R75 friction-fed offset press at 14 Vincent Place, Yeovil. The output of titles had now increased a little as John had hired a former employee of Autobooks to write for him, commencing with what amounted to a handbook on the Ford Anglia. He had perceived a need to get into car workshop manuals because at that time manufacturers such as Ford, Jaguar and Rover would not supply their complex and expensive technical manuals to the general public and nothing else more comprehensive than handbooks was available. The person he took on had permission to use Ford copyright material but, although the idea was sound, the end product left much to be desired. Fate decreed that, only a short while afterwards, the opportunity would present itself for John to create his own workshop manual, and thereby establish the pattern on which the major part of the present business enterprise is founded.

Opportunity came in the guise of Dave Hyland, a fellow RAF officer who had a frog-eye Austin-Healey Sprite out in Aden which required much attention. Willing to help him out, John hit upon the idea of taking the entire car to pieces and rebuilding it, so that practical experience could be gained for the origination of a full-scale workshop manual. Having got his friend's consent, he bought a 35mm Asahi Pentax camera duty free (as Aden was then a freeport), to take all the stage-by-stage photographs that would accompany the text. It was not an easy task working in the heat of Aden, and having to carry the engine up four flights of stairs so that it could be dismantled in the back bedroom of John and Annette's flat. But the project was completed satisfactorily with everyone pitching in, including Annette. In due course the manuscript was posted back to David for printing, the decision having been made to produce it in the new, larger, A4 format, to make the most of the photographs and line drawings.

A breakthrough had been achieved when permission to reproduce Leyland copyright drawings had been granted by the company's Public Relations Officer, one S. A. C. Haynes, surely a good omen. Printing in this format created some problems as far as David was concerned, for the maximum sheet size of his press was only a fraction over A4. In consequence

he had to feed one page at a time through the press, and each sheet required two passes through the press because it could print only one side at a time. After printing, the collating was carried out by their parents at their home, and the binding by a local printer who had this facility. Written in lay terms, the new manual enjoyed excellent reviews in the motoring press, being regarded as something quite exceptional. Of the 3,000 copies printed initially, all were sold within six months. The Haynes *Owners Workshop Manual* had, in modern space-age parlance, achieved 'lift off'. It was the first workshop manual to carry the Haynes imprint, although it was not the first use of the logo. The embryonic logo had first been used on the title page of *Vintage Automobiles*, Vol 1, by H. Thornton Rutter, which John had commissioned in 1965.

Other titles soon followed along similar lines, including those relating to the Austin A35 and A40, the Morris Minor 1000 and the Ford Anglia. David was kept busy, soon having to increase his regular paper order from dozens of reams to a ton at a time, in cut sheet form, to keep pace with demand. Next, he moved to a larger building in South Western Terrace, Yeovil because of the need for more storage and production space, sharing premises with Servu, a small chain of successful auto accessory shops. This was only a temporary measure whilst he looked around for something more permanent that would better suit his and John's requirements. In 1965 he found what he wanted in the form of three terraced cottages at Lower Odcombe, on the outskirts of Yeovil, one of which had once been the village Co-op food shop. With running water and electricity but no drainage, and just a chemical 'privy' at the back, all three could be bought for £1,850 freehold.

The possibility of being able to acquire the Lower Odcombe premises was of sufficient importance for John to request an RAF special low-cost

indulgence flight home, so that he could view them himself. The decision to purchase was made, and David's printing company moved to Lower Odcombe after the necessary alterations had been completed. At the same time, the opportunity was taken to transfer the bookshop to Lower Odcombe, with a Mrs Ferguson who lived nearby to run it on a part-time basis. Sufficient room was made available for David to take up residence in the same premises, but only after they had been given a thorough clean. It proved to be a most distasteful job, as they were filthy and overrun with rats. Some of the rats' tunnels were so long that when smoke bombs were lit to drive them out, smoke was seen emerging from the furthermost end of the building some 15 minutes later, all three cottages having been joined together.

John's posting to Aden came to an end in October 1966, about the time the printing equipment had been installed and was in full operation. He now found himself posted to the Ministry of Defence in Harrogate, Yorkshire, but instead of doing the interesting sort of job with which he had always been involved, such as being in charge of one of the round-the-clock shifts at Khormaksar dealing with moving men and material by air, he found himself desk-bound and doing a very boring job checking never-ending lists of equipment to establish whether stocks were sufficient. It was a far cry from the responsibility for the loading and off-loading of passengers, baggage and freight from aircraft which came from and went to destinations all over the world. After six months of this drudgery he decided that, much as he had enjoyed it earlier, he had seen enough of the RAF and wished to resign his commission so that he could go full time into his publishing business which was now expanding rapidly.

After presenting his case to the Air Secretary of the Air Ministry, it was reluctantly agreed that he would be permitted to retire prematurely, on the

understanding that he would receive no pension and no gratuity. In 1967, and with several months still to go before leaving the RAF, John obtained details of residential property in the Yeovil area, and it was quite by chance that he had the opportunity to purchase one half of Camway House in West Camel, a large, old farmhouse, with Victorian additions, the other half of which had been split into flats. The half he purchased included the adjoining barn, which would offer great potential for the expansion of the printing side of the business if planning permission could be obtained.

The move from Harrogate was made in an aged Bedford CA van, necessitating three separate journeys, in August 1967. Until Camway House was ready for occupation, John and Annette and their first baby, six-month old John Junior (hence JJ, or Jay as he is known outside the family) lived in two rooms on the first floor of the end terrace house at Lower Odcombe. The facility had no bathroom, only cold running water and still no proper toilet, making use of the indoor chemical loo! Ironically, it was at about this time that David Haynes, having served his National Service in the RAF, decided to go back into the force, having got fed up with the long hours he was having to work and the necessity of putting in a seven-day week to build up his one-man printing business. He sold his business to John, who took on Adrian Hopper to run it under its new name, The Odcombe Press, and immediately expanded it by adding an extra Rotaprint R30/90 suction-fed press and more staff.

As the publishing business continued to grow, additional staff were taken on, including Colonel Felix Nicholson as a general assistant. Stanley Randolph, a retired insurance executive, was engaged to run the now re-titled Motorists' Bookshop on a full-time basis and the building was modified so that a bigger process camera could be installed upstairs in a darkroom erected behind the one bedroom. An increasing number of workshop manual orders were now being received from trade sources and it was realised that if the business was to continue to grow, important though the mail order side was, supplying the traditional book trade, with all that followed in the way of

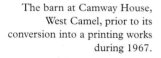

The barn at Camway House, West Camel, prior to its conversion into a printing works during 1967.

opening accounts, raising invoices and so on, would need to be implemented.

Soon after this had happened, John Hall was recruited as salesman during June 1969. Previously, he had worked for Marglass in Sherborne, on the sales side, and not long after his secretary from that company, Margaret Ibbotson, joined him at Lower Odcombe to continue in a similar role. It became the established practice to load John Hall's Vauxhall Victor Estate with books and tell him not to return until all were sold!

At one time a Mark X Jaguar was used for the same purpose, with the passenger's seat removed for extra capacity. This gave rise to the claim that Haynes *Owners Workshop Manuals* had the fastest delivery service of any publisher! Others who joined the company about this time were Rod Grainger, who came in October 1969 as Editorial Assistant, and during 1970,

Narrow country lanes do not aid manoeuvrability, as was evident when it came to off-loading the Rotaprint presses during the move-in to Camway House. There is just room for a fork lift truck to squeeze by.

Inside the print room at Lower Odcombe. Nigel Eade (left) and Stephen Dominey, with the Rotaprint presses.

The first delivery of paper to Camway House from Robert Horne; the beginning of a long association between the two companies in respect of paper supplies.

When deliveries of paper arrived it was all hands to the pump, lifting the packages over the garden wall. John Haynes and John Hall are seen here doing their share of the work.

John Warry to help with the printing, Carol Hillard to assist with the collating and binding work, and John Ridgers who supervised such work delivering loose sheets to outworkers who collated them in their own homes, as John's parents continued to do. It is interesting to reflect that Yeovil was famous for its outworkers when the glove industry was at its height, so that the collating work was the continuation of a local tradition.

As luck would have it, John and Annette Haynes were able to gain full possession of Camway House during 1969, some 18 months after their initial purchase of the half in which they lived. By this time, planning permission had been obtained for the use of the adjoining barn to house the printing equipment, which was moved from Lower Odcombe to leave only the editorial and layout facilities there, as well as the Motorists' Bookshop. The conversion of the barn necessitated the installation of RSJs so that the books could be stored upstairs, without causing structural failure by their weight. At first it seemed as though there was so much space available that it would never get used up. Yet such was the rate of growth of the company that, within another 18 months, there was danger of the barn being over-full.

Sandra MacKinnon joined the company in 1969 and first worked with Annette in Camway House helping with accounts, and a year or so later became secretary to Frank Day, shortly after that becoming John's Personal Secretary, a position she still holds today, her competence and efficiency greatly easing his day-to-day workload.

One of the more important appointments during 1970 had involved Frank Day, when it became obvious that someone was needed to handle the accounts which, until then, had been one of the many tasks carried out by John and Annette Haynes. Within a week of his appointment he was working full-time, taking on additional responsibilities as time progressed that ranged from personnel recruitment to father confessor when anyone was faced with a problem and needed advice; his door was always open and he became a tower of strength in the growing company.

The expansion of production facilities resulted in additional appointments too, and during 1971 they included John Rose as a paste-up artist/camera operator, John Brooks and Tim Snook to help with book despatch and book production respectively, and Nick Cudmore to assist with the platemaking. John Brooks married Sally White who had aided Annette as a mother's help for several years, a second son, Marc, having been born in April 1968, so everything was becoming very busy.

2

A move to Sparkford

In September 1971, with the premises at Lower Odcombe and West Camel full to overflowing, it was with the greatest of excitement that John and Annette Haynes saw, on return from their first trip to the USA, while driving through the village of Sparkford, that the huge Unigate creamery was up for sale. Only a couple of miles from West Camel, Sparkford is mid-way between London and Land's End, straddling the old A303 which was by-passed in 1989 by a new dual carriageway that forms part of the improved main road to the west. Travelling in the opposite direction, London is about 120 miles away and about two hours' driving time from the village.

Immediate enquiries were put in hand regarding the creamery. When it was learned how little (compared with new units on trading estates) was wanted for the freehold of this 30,000 square foot building, a deal was swiftly concluded, much to the amazement of Unigate who could not imagine why anyone should want an old milk processing factory on a sloping site right next to the railway line and in the middle of a rural village in Somerset. Not immediately suited to the requirements of a printer and publisher, it nonetheless represented a good acquisition – a proven fact since, 29 years and much experience later, the Haynes Publishing Group still operates from those same premises which are its headquarters.

One of the few pieces of equipment the company took over from the creamery was a very old Crossley six-cylinder, 12-litre diesel engine coupled to a 68.8kVA three-phase 400-volt generator. Subsequently, the engine was overhauled and rebuilt (the unit was so old that only one person in England had spare parts for it), and it proved an absolute godsend during the power cuts that occurred during the miners' strike of 1974. The engine ran at a steady 1,000rpm and it was a grand sight to see all the lights on at the Sparkford factory when all around was plunged into inky darkness. The addition of new production equipment eventually made it redundant when it was no longer able to meet the increased electrical demand.

Although substantial internal alterations were necessary to make the building better suited to the requirements of its new occupants, some of them proved easier than others. For instance, the large area on the ground floor at

The Sparkford creamery prior to its acquisition and occupation during 1972. The green-painted water tank on the roof was a familiar landmark to motorists on the A303.

This photograph shows the depth of the premises, not readily apparent to passers-by on the road. The railway line is still in use, forming a link between Castle Cary and Weymouth, via Yeovil. The remains of the old siding into the factory are still evident today.

the rear of the building proved relatively easy to convert into the workshop where vehicles could be stripped and rebuilt for manual projects. There were already the makings of an inspection pit in the form of a sunken bay in which milk churns had been washed out and cleaned before they left the factory to be re-used. Furthermore, the wall adjacent to the canopied side entrance that ran parallel to the railway line was equipped with large roller shutter doors, which allowed access for even quite large vehicles. It was this area that formed the core of every workshop manual project, and the cornerstone on which the success of these publications was firmly based, because no one previously had gone through a complete stripdown and rebuild routine of vehicles for every single title, with the author, photographer and trained mechanic working in close co-operation.

Right from the very beginning it had been John's policy to write from first-hand practical experience, so that attention could be drawn to any difficulties or problems likely to be encountered by the average DIY enthusiast who was determined to tackle his own maintenance and repairs. Innumerable photographs and line drawings keyed into the text made the

The motorcycle manuals project commenced during late 1972. Here, Brian Horsfall (left) and Jeff Clew are seen dismantling a BSA Bantam engine. This formed the basis of the third motorcycle title to be published.

stage-by-stage operations easy to follow, the author writing in plain, easy-to-understand terms. Equally important was the determination not to use special service tools unless they were considered to be absolutely essential. Inevitably there are ways and means of pulling parts off and replacing them again afterwards, without risk of damage, by resorting to ingenious methods of improvisation, and there had never been any lack of these. In consequence the workshop did not contain a sophisticated display of tools, but only those that would be found in the average toolkit. Photographic evidence was always available to prove to even the most hardened of disbelievers that these techniques worked.

By now, the workshop routine had fallen into a familiar pattern, very similar to that employed when the frog-eye Austin-Healey Sprite was stripped and rebuilt in Aden for the very first *Owners Workshop Manual*, but with just a modicum of 'fine tuning' here and there. The decision was made fairly early on to omit automatic transmissions and not to include details of how to dismantle a differential, as ultra-clean conditions are needed for the former, to say nothing of the need for a degree of information that would justify

Car manual projects continued alongside those of the motorcycles. Brian Horsfall prepares the removal of a Volvo engine while author Peter Strasman provides encouragement.

virtually a complete workshop manual in itself, and complicated special tools with which correctly to set up the latter. Everything else was covered in a very thorough manner.

Externally, the appearance of the building took on a new look when the old 10,000 gallon water tank on the roof was cut up and removed from its supports. It had served as a familiar landmark for travellers who had used the A303 when it passed through the village.

The official opening of the premises took place on 22 November 1972, just one month after the birth to John and Annette of a third son, who was named Christopher. By now all the printing, editorial, layout and clerical staff had been installed there. Only the Motorists' Bookshop remained at Lower Odcombe, and Camway House had reverted to private residential use. Representatives from the motoring press and the local newspaper were invited to a guided tour of the premises, preceded by a lunch, those journalists who needed to travel from London having the option of a journey by a coach that was specially chartered for the occasion.

Unfortunately its departure was much delayed through waiting for latecomers and since those on board not unnaturally took advantage of a free bar, the result was that quite a few were decidedly 'under the weather' by the time the coach arrived at Sparkford! However, all went well in the end and

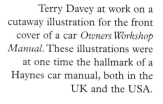

Terry Davey at work on a cutaway illustration for the front cover of a car *Owners Workshop Manual*. These illustrations were at one time the hallmark of a Haynes car manual, both in the UK and the USA.

some useful column inches were gained in the more popular motoring magazines. In addition, the local newspaper ran a special two-page feature, explaining the unique way in which the manuals were originated.

Coinciding with the move of all the remaining staff to Sparkford was the start of the *Motorcycle Owners Workshop Manual* project, the idea being to begin producing manuals for motorcycles as a parallel operation and in the same way as the car manuals. Jeff Clew joined J. H. Haynes & Co Ltd late in 1972 to get it under way, his previous experience in handling the publicity and technical writing for an instrument company in Brighton and the authorship of two motorcycling books proving of much help in his new job. With the car workshop manuals already well established, there was evidence of a real need for motorcycle manuals bearing the Haynes imprint and this, coupled with the way in which the books had been received by the motor trade, made it not too difficult to convince even the most sceptical that the day of the DIY *Motorcycle Owners Workshop Manual* had arrived.

Just one major problem remained – how to obtain machines to strip and rebuild when the Haynes name and the concept of a really comprehensive workshop manual were virtually unknown in the motorcycle trade. Few were willing to entrust one of their machines into what they regarded as unskilled hands, while some held the popular misconception that the availability of relatively low-cost DIY manuals would undermine their repair business. Similar problems had been encountered when the car manuals started, so initially, as in the case of the cars, machines were purchased privately after scanning newspapers and magazines, then re-sold at the conclusion of the project at a small but useful profit.

Eventually, one or two of the local dealers realised the business

Gill Carroll checks a paste-up in the layout room, the black 'windows' indicating the position of the photographs that will accompany the text. This is a far cry from the on-screen computer technology that is used today for page make-up.

Just as important was the work of the Sales Department, where customer orders had to be filled and invoiced. Rita Hill operates the Burroughs computer – the modern tecnology of the day, and again, a great contrast to today's hi-tech systems.

potential and offered their help, to form a link that still exists today. When Haynes manuals began to get more firmly established amongst motorcyclists, manufacturers and concessionaires offered their assistance too. The first three motorcycle titles were launched at the Waldorf Hotel, London, on 12 April 1973, but the real breakthrough occurred when Suzuki (Great Britain) Ltd purchased all the Haynes Suzuki titles to sell through their own Spares Department. This provided the much-needed 'stamp of approval' from a major manufacturer and the new motorcycle manuals were well and truly on their way.

By this time the 50th car manual title had been published in February 1973, on the Renault 4. The total number of books of all kinds being printed and bound now amounted to an average of 8,000 copies per week, with printing taking place on four offset litho presses. To help realise this output, a team of authors had been built up, all of whom were experts on cars, to bring the total workforce up to 60.

The Motorists' Bookshop at Lower Odcombe was the last part of the operation to be moved to Sparkford and was installed during the early part of 1973. Betty Hill took over the running of the shop from Stanley Randolph and organised its development and growth. Originally, the bookshop had stocked a very wide range of motoring and motorcycling books from many different publishers, but as the company's output increased, there was soon only enough shelf space to stock Haynes titles exclusively. As the workload increased, and Betty became more and more involved with the day-to-day running of the Despatch Department, a Bookshop Manager had to be appointed.

Customers calling at the bookshop created a problem by their indiscriminate parking alongside a busy road, which caused the Parish Council much concern. Despite concerted attempts to get them to use the company's own car park, all notices were ignored. One driver actually knocked down a 'no parking' sign while manoeuvring into position, and another tried to drive through the bookshop window!

Clearly these were exciting times, the immediate objective being to build up as quickly as possible, a range of workshop manuals that would match the range of the market leader and major competitor, Autobooks, so that the market could be wrested away. But in attempting to achieve this it was important not to compromise in any way the manuals' own unique selling point, in the knowledge that research and origination costs were of necessity high in following this path. Too much attention could not be given to advertising and marketing until the range was complete and an open attack could be made on the opposition in the understanding that Haynes had the better product. With limited resources everything had to be put into the product to bridge that vital gap. Behind it all was the determination to have a better product at a competitive price, properly advertised and marketed, and backed up by a delivery and distribution service that would overwhelm the opposition completely.

3

Acquisition and expansion:
successes and disasters

In the early 1960s, when the company was virtually a two-man band, it had been decided that the Sporting Motorists' Bookshop would sell motoring books from other publishers. Some publishers, such as B. T. Batsford, happily gave the necessary trade discount of 33⅓ per cent, but the UK's then-leading publisher of motoring books, G. T. Foulis & Co Ltd, was not so happy to follow suit. It took a visit by John Haynes to the company's offices at 1–5 Portpool Lane, London EC1 to persuade Miles Marshall, a somewhat stern-looking, up-market publisher, that the Sporting Motorists' Bookshop was worthy to carry a stock of such high quality motoring books. Even then, the most discount that could be allowed was 25 per cent.

By a strange twist of fate it was during 1973, not long after everyone had moved into Sparkford, that the opportunity presented itself for the company to buy G. T. Foulis. It came about because their directors had decided that with one of them in his seventies and another in his sixties, the time had come to consider retirement. And so one of Britain's oldest publishing houses, a company with a prestigious imprint and a history that extended back over 400 years, was put up for sale. Harold and Miles Marshall were cousins and ran the business on delightfully old-fashioned lines, even to maintaining a hand-written postage book. Anxious to break into the book trade and at the same time broaden his company's interests, John made a successful bid, the agreement to buy being completed on 2 July 1973. The Foulis list contained some classic motoring titles, such as Hans Tanner's *Ferrari* and Hugh Conway's *Bugatti*, and it so happened that this latter title was the first to be reprinted at the Sparkford premises.

With the need to put so much time and energy into the production of workshop manuals in order to have a range of titles that would match that of the company's main competitor, it may be questioned why this diversification into acquiring another company took place at this time.

The underlying reasons are not difficult to understand. Quite apart from the excellent back list of G. T. Foulis which contained many highly desirable titles now regarded as classics, to buy such a prestigious company was not just a feather in John's cap but also a means of adding to the profitability

Moving in new equipment often causes problems, in this case necessitating knocking a hole in a wall! A new Kolbus EMP casing-in machine is manoeuvred into position after its off-loading by crane.

of J. H. Haynes & Co Ltd. Being a motoring enthusiast and a book publisher too, John could not turn down the chance of acquiring such an interesting company. The price was fair and it was a move that would take the company into the world of traditional book publishing so that it would no longer be a one-product-line business. So, although most effort continued to be put into the production and publication of *Owners Workshop Manuals*, G. T. Foulis was taken over as a running entity, with all the extra work which that implied.

As the whole company of G. T. Foulis was being taken over, including the non-motoring books, the creditors and debtors, and all the work in progress, it was agreed that Miles Marshall, the younger of the two cousins, would continue for a number of months. Towards the end of the take-over transition period, it was agreed with John Hassell, the third director of G. T. Foulis and the editor who dealt with the non-motoring titles, that his publishing interest would be relinquished. Mostly, these titles were more in the nature of scientific treatises on subjects remote from motoring, and correspondingly few in number. But for all that they were regarded as definitive works and went on selling steadily in small numbers for many years.

Incorporating the G. T. Foulis books raised several new problems, not the least of which was the need to break into an entirely new market. Whereas most of the workshop manuals were now sold to the motor accessory trade or by mail order, the G. T. Foulis titles had to be sold into bookshops. There was also the need to commission new motoring titles and to add some motorcycling titles to the list. To overcome these problems, Tim Parker and Jeff Clew were given the responsibility of seeking out new manuscripts and encouraging existing authors to consider updating their works that were already in print, and the sales force was restructured. At that time, the company did not have its own full-time salesmen but relied upon freelance agents, who of their own choice, represented from eight to twelve companies, one of which was J. H. Haynes & Co Ltd. None of the companies they represented had conflicting interests, and the representatives' incomes were derived solely from the commission they earned. It was a system that worked well at the time, so much so that two of the original agents were still working for the company twelve years later on a full-time basis.

Overall responsibility for sales rested with John Hall in his capacity of Sales Manager, soon to be appointed to the Board as Sales Director. To help him he had as his assistant George Magnus, a young former G. T. Foulis employee who was learning the book trade and had joined the staff at Sparkford at the time of the takeover. When John Hall left to settle in California and run the US operation, George stayed on, firstly as assistant to Geoff Cowen, who had succeeded John Hall. When Geoff left, George decided to become a sales representative and joined Graham Wade (one of Haynes's manufacturer's agents), but many years later rejoined the company in 1996 as UK Sales Director. After Geoff's departure, Terry Egan had been appointed Sales Manager. As detailed in the following chapter, he developed a full-time sales force, retaining only two of the original freelance agents, who sold to both the motor accessory trade and to the traditional bookshop outlets.

History has a habit of repeating itself and when the Oxford Illustrated Press was acquired much later, in 1981, it then became apparent that the traditional bookshop outlets would require much stronger representation, especially as the output from G. T. Foulis had increased considerably by that time. Although the former Oxford Illustrated Press representatives had been retained for this purpose, it soon became obvious that only by recruiting a team of full-time bookshop representatives could the necessary impact be achieved. The new bookshop sales force became fully operational during 1983 and almost immediately the increased sales that resulted proved beyond all doubt that this had been the correct action to take.

The acquisition of G. T. Foulis did not have its effect on sales and marketing alone. Production had to face a number of changes too, because it was no longer a question of producing what amounted to a standard product, each successive workshop manual following a prescribed route. Whilst the IBM typesetting had proved quite adequate for this type of work, the quality

The casing-in machine is eased down wooden ramps towards its final resting place. Alec Rollo watches progress anxiously.

of its printed impression left much to be desired in the case of 'quality' books which would have a sewn, cloth binding. There was also the need to have available a number of different typefaces, and in various point sizes, and even varying grades of paper, depending on whether or not the book was heavily illustrated. The answer to the first part of the problem lay in the introduction of computerised photo-typesetting, which provided the degree of flexibility desired and at the same time would speed up production. A certain amount of retraining proved necessary, with regard to both the typesetters and the editors, now that more precise mark-up instructions needed to be given and fully understood. Paper grades were not so much a problem as a question of extra expense, together with the need for more storage space in conditions where the paper would not suffer unduly from the effects of humidity.

Changes occurred editorially, too. Soon after Jeff Clew had been appointed to the J. H. Haynes Board as Editorial Director in December 1978, and Rod Grainger had been appointed Managing Editor of G. T. Foulis, Jeff was appointed also a director of G. T. Foulis. As the workload grew during the months that followed, and the output of new titles increased considerably, it was soon obvious that some further rearrangement was necessary. This occurred during June 1979 when Rod Grainger was appointed to the G. T. Foulis Board, an appointment which led to his later promotion to Managing Editorial Director. By that time, Foulis was already buying in a number of foreign co-published and packaged titles on a very selective basis (to supplement those that had been originated in-house) and was also involved in book club transactions which enabled print runs to be increased substantially. To cope with all this extra work, a Production Editor was sought, and this vacancy was filled internally by Mansur Darlington, who changed allegiance from editing *Motorcycle Owners Workshop Manuals* in October 1983.

The output of G. T. Foulis titles not only increased considerably as time progressed but also had its coverage broadened by books on diverse subjects such as bicycles, aircraft and railway locomotives. The DIY theme was later expanded by titles covering subjects ranging from powered lawnmowers to washing machines and similar domestic appliances, and even the maintenance of oil-fired central heating systems. Especially popular was a new range of titles about the buying and DIY restoration of some of the more popular mass-produced cars, which as the Haynes *Restoration Manual* series continues to be expanded to the present day. Other popular, long-life books covered engine preparation and tuning for competition work. Also published was one of the first books to cover virtually every aspect of BMX bicycles.

It was during the autumn of 1980 that John Haynes became aware of the well-reviewed motoring books in the *Classic Car* series that were being produced by the Oxford Illustrated Press. At that time, the publishing industry was going through a difficult spell, and in talking to Chris Harvey, a G. T. Foulis author who was also the author of some of the OIP *Classic Cars* titles, it became apparent that these Oxford-based publishers were having problems. He made a point of meeting Jane Marshall, their Editorial Director, at the 1980 London Book Fair, and arranged to visit her during the winter after his return from a visit to California.

Over lunch, it was realised that Jane *was* Oxford Illustrated Press, being responsible for all aspects of its successful running. The company was owned by Blackwells, whose name is synonymous with Oxford, and due to the overall recession in the book trade it appeared they would be amenable to an offer if one were to be made.

Aware that John probably would be seriously interested because of the excellent range of motoring titles on her list, Jane had all the facts and figures available at her fingertips. Negotiations commenced and by March 1981 the Oxford Illustrated Press had been purchased from Blackwells, with Jane continuing as Editorial Director but working from her home instead of the small Nissen hut in Shelley Road that had been used previously. With only a

BBC Television showed great interest in the unique way in which Haynes Manuals were originated. Here, John Norman of their Bristol studio looks at the way in which a Suzuki motorcycle was completely dismantled, for a spot in their 'Points West' evening programme.

ITV was just as interested too. This is Laurie Quayle of Westward Television interviewing Frank Day for 'Westward Diary'. In the foreground is a stripped Honda Accord gearbox.

part-time typist to help her, the reduced overheads meant that OIP soon became profitable and continued to be so for many years as new titles were added to the back list.

For John personally, the acquisition of OIP marked a period of considerable growth of knowledge of how the traditional book trade operates because when G. T. Foulis had been acquired much earlier, no one had come over from the editorial side. Experience in selling translation rights to foreign publishers, as well as rights to paperback houses and book clubs had, until then, been lacking at Sparkford, so familiarisation with these and similar activities led directly to a considerable increase in turnover and growth of G. T. Foulis.

The Oxford Illustrated Press list contained some 35 separate book titles, including nine up-market motoring books that would fit in well with the Haynes range. It also provided the opportunity for some further diversification of interest because the list contained books on topics such as cookery, art, travel and adventure.

As mentioned earlier, the acquisition of the Oxford Illustrated Press led

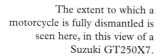

The extent to which a motorcycle is fully dismantled is seen here, in this view of a Suzuki GT250X7.

The sale of translation rights has played an important part in obtaining market penetration overseas. These are just two examples of motorcycle manuals sold in Germany and Holland. It may seem strange that an English language BMW manual should be translated into German!

to the need to recruit a full-time sales force with the necessary experience of selling directly to the traditional book trade. The success of this move became apparent very soon in the number of new bookshop accounts that were opened and in the increase in orders that resulted. All sales representatives had a regular calling cycle within their area, taking with them the very latest advance information on new titles to help generate pre-publication sales.

A further acquisition took place during May 1983 when 18 motoring titles were obtained from Gentry Books, all of a very specialised nature which would fit in well with the Foulis list but which that imprint probably would not have published on their own. The Managing Director of Gentry Books had decided to become more involved with travel books and to sponsor publications, so to raise the cash for this he agreed, after coming to an amicable arrangement, to sell the rights to the motoring titles, the stock and the film, and also the logo. It was, however, merely a case of plugging a few gaps in the Foulis list, as there was no intention to add more Gentry titles but merely to update and reprint the existing titles under the G. T. Foulis imprint as they went out of stock.

So far, it would seem that everything had gone according to plan as far as acquisitions were concerned, negotiations progressing smoothly and quickly, and expansion occurring at a rate that often exceeded even the most optimistic of expectations. True though this was, it would be quite wrong to create the impression that this had always been so without exception, for there was one attempt at diversification into magazine publishing that had amounted to a complete disaster.

During May 1982 two young men, Ian Bamsey and Philip Bingham, came to John Haynes with a proposition to publish both an up-market monthly motor sporting magazine and also a motorsport yearbook. They suggested that if the necessary backing were provided, a new company would be created within the Haynes Publishing Group to publish the magazine and the yearbook and that they would become directors of that company to run the magazine and edit the yearbook.

After discussions had taken place, it was agreed to finance the project and that Ian Bamsey would commence work with the Group prior to the formation of the new company – Automobile Sport Limited – on 1 June 1982. Projections provided by Ian and Philip suggested the total risk capital would amount to £50,000 and that while the new magazine, to be called *Automobile Sport*, would lose money up to a maximum of approximately £37,500 during the first seven months of publication, thereafter cashflow would be positive until such time as the deficit had been amortised and the magazine was making a regular profit.

Offices for the magazine were provided at Ivel House, Ilchester, and a secretary/editorial assistant taken on, an advertising agency, John Leonard Associates, appointed to handle much of the promotion and related work and to assist with the initial launch. Meanwhile, advertisements were being placed for an Advertising Manager. The decision to have the magazine typeset and printed outside the Group had already been taken and it had also been agreed that the distribution would be undertaken by a specialist in the magazine field, who would sell direct to newsagents on a sale or return basis as is the customary practice. The close proximity of the 1982 Motor Show at the National Exhibition Centre in Birmingham suggested this would provide the ideal opportunity and venue for the launch to take place. At this stage, only 12–15 pages of advertising had been sold against an expectation of 20, but the launch went ahead as planned, the typesetting and printing having been carried out by Lawrence Allen, a firm in Weston-super-Mare.

Some disquieting facts emerged during the first board meeting of Automobile Sport Ltd after the launch. After Ian Bamsey had stated that the distributors had reported sales of approximately 51 per cent of the first issue, which had a 60,000-copy print run at their recommendation, the cashflow projections provided by David Haynes (Group Company Secretary and Finance Director since rejoining the business in 1981) showed a total expenditure of £75,000 on the production of the first issue. At the following board meeting held three weeks later, the loss for the year to date already amounted to £43,000, with only two issues published. The shortfall in advertising revenue had been a major contributory factor to this deficit and it was obvious that every effort needed to be made to expand the advertisement section from 20 to 36 pages. With no success in finding an Advertising Manager, the telephone sales girl who had been taken on for a three-month period to work on a commission basis was asked to continue to sell advertising space on a part-time basis while more strenuous efforts were made to fill the vacancy.

Circulation figures showed that readership was falling, from 32,000 in the case of the first issue to 28,000 by the time the third issue had appeared and a probable 25,000 for the fourth. Print runs had been trimmed accordingly but although the Group's maximum investment had by now far exceeded the original maximum risk projection, the appointment of Nick Hervey as Advertising Manager on 7 February 1983 suggested the situation from then on should begin to improve. Sadly it did not and by May that year the deficit had grown to an alarming size, although at this point the slate was wiped clean as it was considered the sums expended represented an 'investment' in getting the magazine off the ground.

The magazine continued to lose money and at the end of the first quarter the point had been reached where drastic remedial action needed to be taken. The magazine could still prove to be a success, but only if expenses were cut significantly. In the resultant rearrangement, Ian Bamsey and Philip Bingham resigned their directorships and Ian left Automobile Sport Limited, Brian Laban, a well-known journalist, being offered the post of Managing Editor and the responsibilities of Nick Hervey increased. In view of his intimate involvement with the accounts of the company, Peter Bishop was appointed Accounts Director, in addition to the other directorships he held within the Haynes Publishing Group at that time.

Production of the July 1983 issue was completed virtually on schedule to avoid a break in continuity, but at the expense of some loss of advertising due to unforeseen problems with copy date deadlines. The August issue appeared more or less on time too, so that the magazine could be promoted at Silverstone from the company's Motorhome.

Arrangements were made for Derek Warwick to sign copies of the magazine and for Derek Bell to sign 24 copies of the *Automobile Sport Yearbook* as part of the promotional campaign. The promotion proved a great success from the advertising point of view and a similar promotion was arranged for the British and European Grand Prix at Brands Hatch in September.

Despite the rearrangement of publishing schedules to give the magazine a more favourable lead-in time so that eventually it would be published on the 20th of the month preceding the cover date, there was still no sign of the positive cashflow that by now was long overdue.

When the Annual General Meeting of Automobile Sport Limited was held on 20 October 1983 there was only one decision that could be made; it was unanimously agreed to suspend publication of the magazine and try to find a buyer for it. Ian Bamsey bought back the rights to the *Automobile Sport Yearbook* for a nominal sum and Brian Laban bought *Automobile Sport* magazine – which by then had lost nearly £250,000 – for the value of its assets, a question of a few thousand pounds. Closing the magazine was a bitter pill for John Haynes to swallow, but he could see no way in which it would come into profit.

Inevitably there were lessons to be learnt from this setback, not the least of which was the considerable differences that exist between book

Book launches have helped to promote many book trade titles. Racing driver Jody Scheckter autographs copies of his biography, published under the G.T. Foulis imprint, at a signing session in London. Left, Mandy Jeans, right, John Haynes.

publishing and magazine publishing. In the latter deadlines are very strict and *must* be met if sales are not to suffer severely.

Furthermore, the success of a magazine depends very much on the advertising revenue it generates. Perhaps of even more importance in this instance was the fact that all the rules upon which the Group business had been founded had been broken by not retaining full control of editorial, production and distribution. If any good came out of the closure of the magazine, it was the realisation that when set financial parameters have been broken, work should cease immediately and not be allowed to continue, incurring ever-increasing losses. Had *Automobile Sport* been stopped after the second or third issues, the loss incurred would have been about a quarter of the eventual total. It showed that the company could be just as fallible as any other company when decisions are made and that personal enthusiasm can sometimes cloud judgement. To quote John's own words 'In future I shall stick to books!'

A further addition to the Haynes Publishing Group of companies took place during January 1984 when Camway Autographics was formed to handle all the Group's advertising and public relations activities as well as the design and erection of stands at trade and retail shows. It was formed in accordance with John's basic operating principle of vertical integration whenever possible, so that all the work is contained within the Group without need to use outside contractors unless absolutely essential. Direct benefits were soon achieved by taking advantage of the discounts given to advertising agencies by magazines and newspapers. David Hermelin, who joined Camway Autographics from the company's former advertising agents, John Leonard Associates, was appointed a director of the new company as was Murray Corfield, the Group's former Marketing Manager.

4

Consolidation and growth at Sparkford

One of the areas to expand most at Sparkford was the Print Room. When the printing equipment was moved there from West Camel during September 1972, only two Rotaprints had to be transported, to which were added a further press, a folding machine, a three-knife trimmer, a binder and a gatherer. A Heidelberg Kord printing press was purchased at the same time, so that full-colour printing could be handled in-house. The production staff had now increased to 20, under the control of Brian Lugg who had been recruited earlier that year as Printing Manager. Within the next couple of years, two more Rotaprints were acquired and new equipment installed so that the car manuals could be bound in a hard plastic cover. Further changes in 1975 necessitated the installation of a casemaking machine, the plastic covers having been superseded by card covers of a more pleasing appearance. So that the new covers could be printed in-house, a Heidelberg Sorm colour printing press was purchased.

In May 1973 Ivel House in Ilchester had been acquired, part of which

Ivel House, Ilchester, during occupation by the Haynes Publishing Group. The lower floor had previously been a café/restaurant in the days when the A303 passed through the village.

at one time had been a cafe in the days when the A303 passed through the centre of the village. Located about six miles west of Sparkford, the building served admirably to accommodate overflow from the main site, to become the temporary home of a number of different departments after the inevitable refurbishment had been completed.

Space in the Print Room was now at a premium, so the entire colour printing operation was transferred to the ground floor of Ivel House and augmented by the addition of a second Kord press. During the summer of 1976 the first two-colour press, a Miller, was installed at Ilchester, along with a laminating machine, to dispense with the need to have workshop manual covers clad in clear plastic film by an outside contractor. Now that more room was available in the Print Room at Sparkford, a much larger binding machine, a three-knife trimmer and an in-line casing-in machine were purchased early in 1977 as a prelude to stepping up production. Production control was in the hands of Alec Rollo, who had joined the company as Works Manager in January 1973 and who later became responsible to Mike Yorke, who joined in June 1975 as Production Executive, became General Manager just over a year later and in January 1977 was appointed to the Board as Works Director. The production team was further strengthened by the appointment of Roger Stagg in August 1977 as Production Assistant, bringing with him, like the others, a considerable amount of printing expertise.

Part of the dismantled Miller two-colour press is moved into the Ilchester Print Room prior to its reassembly.

Apart from all the extra work that followed from the acquisition of G. T. Foulis, the output of workshop manuals had increased considerably in terms of both new titles and updates. On the car side, the increased output of manuscripts came from four full-time authors, Brian Chalmers-Hunt, Bill Kinchin, John Larminie and David Stead, with occasional help from others including John Hall, who was then Sales Manager, and Tim Parker, who co-ordinated the efforts of the editorial team and edited their manuscripts in his role of Managing Editor. Car handbooks were written by Pete Ward, who worked from home on a freelance basis, commencing in May 1973. He also dealt with customer enquiries. When the workload became too great for one person to edit, Rod Grainger was appointed Car Workshop Manual Editor in May 1975. On the motorcycle side Jeff Clew, now Motorcycle Books Editor, had taken on freelance authors to increase output.

When space problems confronted the Editorial Department in 1976, it too was moved to Ilchester, into the upstairs portion of Ivel House. The illustrators moved there at the same time, as well as the library, the latter to be run by Reg Hawkins, a local car enthusiast. Sharing a common interest in old vehicles he and Jeff Clew, with John Haynes's blessing, organised three annual old vehicle events locally that were well supported.

Whilst at Ilchester the motorcycle editorial team took on its own full-time authors, the first being Mansur Darlington, one of the original freelancers. They were following the precedent set by the car authors, already working on a full-time basis, but from their homes. An entirely new team had been recruited which included Pete Ward, who had changed from being a freelance to a full-time car manuals author in June 1975. The Editorial Department remained at Ilchester for about 18 months, before further reorganisation at Sparkford created the space needed for its return. There had been many instances of amusement at Ilchester, often when visitors or customers tried to find the entrance to the department, which was hidden round the back of the building and not too clearly marked. Sometimes they would appear unexpectedly at the French windows of an office on the first floor, with a somewhat apprehensive expression, having climbed the fire escape and walked across the flat roof!

The Typesetting Department was another area that had seen dramatic changes take place. Under the control of Annette Pearce in 1973, IBM 'golf ball' electric typewriters were being used to take advantage of their proportional spacing capability and the ease with which point size or typeface could be changed by swapping golf balls. The printed impression they gave was adequate for workshop manuals but not for books that would carry the G. T. Foulis imprint. The answer lay in photo-typesetting, using 'blind' keyboards to produce a coded, punched tape, that could be run off in a computerised processor. It was an expensive but necessary change that involved retraining the operators and a more detailed mark-up from the editors. More output from typesetting meant increased proofreading and film checks, so a full-time proofreader was taken on during September 1977 to look out for literals as well as typographicals, and another person, Gil Kirk, to carry out the final film checks prior to platemaking and printing. By this time, Annette Pearce had left and Paul Young had taken over as Typesetting Manager during October 1977.

The knock-on effect in the form of increasing orders for an ever-widening variety of titles meant more staff in the Sales Office and Accounts Department, to ensure prompt handling and invoicing. When Peter Bishop joined the company in November 1973 to take much of the burden of accounts from Frank Day, part of his duties included sales invoicing and cash collection, with a need to improve on the simple book-keeping system in use at that time. The company's first computer, an electro-mechanical Burroughs L5, was used to process orders, invoices and wages and handle the purchase ledger, 1974 seeing the introduction of the early stages of a manual costing system. The rapid expansion of the company in the mid-1970s placed sufficient additional burdens on the sales office and accounts staff to make further appointments necessary. Les Purcell joined in October 1976 as Sales Office Manager, to take on the responsibility for order entry, sales invoicing, credit control and other related duties. The original Burroughs computer was now proving too slow, so it was replaced in June 1977 by two electro-mechanical Burroughs L900 computers. Because there was a growing need for management information, Alan Sperring joined in September that year as Cost Accountant.

It will be recalled that one of Frank Day's many tasks was that of personnel recruitment and selection, which by the mid-seventies had become a full-time job in itself to say nothing of the need to negotiate with trade unions and administer the company's sickness and pension schemes. As he now held the key position of Managing Director, the need to ease some of his burden was long overdue, so an advertisement was placed for a Personnel Manager, which was filled by Terry Mitchell in August 1977. More or less coincident with his appointment was that of Robin Wager, who had been taken on as Car Handbooks Editor to reactivate this series of publications.

The opportunity to purchase the old Clarks shoe factory at Goldcroft, in Yeovil, made it possible to move the Despatch Department there during March 1976, as recounted in the next chapter. The company was now operating from three different sites, giving rise to stretched lines of communication and the increasing use of transportation. The long-term alternative seemed to be the erection of a new purpose-built factory somewhere in the immediate neighbourhood, so that eventually everything could be brought together again under one roof. That is, until a twist of fate made available Home Farm and some of its land when its elderly occupant died. It was put up for auction on 29 October 1976, split into a number of parcels of land.

Abutting the Sparkford factory, the farmyard had often been looked at longingly when expansion problems began to become acute, and with the prospect of being able to acquire the farmhouse building itself and the immediate farm area of about 3½ acres John Haynes lost no time in taking an interest. With the knowledge that it was well-known in Yeovil that the company was becoming desperately short of space, he was aware that there could well be an attempt to force up the price, so he had his own valuation made which suggested a figure in the region of £30,000.

A local company was appointed auctioneers and on the day it was a nerve-wracking few minutes when £30,000 was reached and John stopped bidding. The price continued to rise, the auctioneer getting more and more excited, saying he was surprised that no one else was coming back into the bidding. When £47,500 appeared to have been reached, he banged his gavel on the table and declared 'not sold', much to John Haynes's relief. Having taken the precaution of having both his lawyer and his accountant present, to enable a deal to be agreed if the property did not sell, he met the auctioneers immediately afterwards and settled on a real purchase price of £31,500.

No time was lost in submitting a planning application for the conversion of the farmhouse into offices and the use of some of the farm outbuildings for industrial purposes, following a vast amount of repair and renovation work. Whilst this would go some way towards the easing of the accommodation problems, more ambitious long-term plans were made for the erection of a purpose-built 10,000 square foot extension to the factory on the old farmyard. In the meanwhile, the two old piggeries at the far end of the newly acquired land were joined together and converted into a large warehouse-cum-raw materials store, which provided 9,000 square feet of accommodation at under £3 per square foot.

The new trimming and binding equipment installed in the Print Room early in 1977 was needed to handle the increased output expected from the

The early stages in the conversion of the two separate wooden piggeries into one large warehouse, shortly after the acquisition of Home Farm in 1978. Clearly a winter-time conversion, as evidenced by the landscape.

Harris web offset press that had been ordered at the same time so that workshop manuals could be printed more rapidly from a continuous reel of paper, 16 pages at a time, then folded as a complete section. Room was needed for the new press, which was due to be installed during June, so the Rotaprints were moved to the outbuilding at Home Farm which previously had been the milking parlour and cow stalls, the interior having been stripped out and made ready. No sooner had the presses been installed and commenced running than the local planning authority got wind of what was going on and decreed all printing operations in that area must stop completely within a month. There seemed no immediate way out until it was realised the Goldcroft factory was very substantially built and could accommodate the Rotaprints on the first floor with a little rearrangement of the Southern Area Distribution Depot that was already in occupation.

The chance to purchase additional premises in Yeovil occurred early in 1978, when Edwin Snell Printers vacated their factory on the corner of Park Road and Clarence Street. The purchase was completed during March and, after internal alterations, the first floor was occupied by the Sales Office and the Accounts Department, their move from Sparkford permitting the Editorial Department to return from Ilchester. The first wages clerk was appointed about this time, made necessary by the increase in the number of employees. Those who moved to Park Road considered they were likely to lead a more tranquil existence, away from the hustle and bustle of Sparkford, but this subsequently proved to be anything but true. Within months of arriving there, the possibility of the company going public arose and the reporting and investigating accountants were with the Accounts Department

The arrival of the first Harris web offset press at Sparkford, room having been created by moving the colour printing to Ilchester. Alan Howden, who maintained all the printing equipment, stands by to help with its installation.

The Southern Area Distribution Depot soon after its move to the former Clarks shoe factory in Goldcroft, Yeovil.

The Southern Area Distribution Depot was transferred to the ground floor of Park Road, Yeovil, in March 1978, to make room for a second print line at Goldcroft. This building was formerly occupied by Edwin Snell Printers.

for many months, the opening of the financial archives for the past five years proving a daunting task. Peter Bishop received the recognition he deserved by his appointment to the Board of J. H. Haynes & Co Ltd in October 1979, to assume responsibility for all accounting functions.

The ground floor of the Park Road premises had been marked out and made ready for the transfer of the Southern Area Distribution Depot from Goldcroft, which also took place during March 1978. As soon as the warehouse staff and stock had left Goldcroft, the Rotaprints that remained there were joined by all the colour printing equipment transferred from Ilchester. During this move, the opportunity was taken to replace the original colour press by a faster Sorm Z two-colour machine and a second binding line was added in December 1979. One further addition, another Heidelberg colour press, represented the last major printing machine purchase before the final move back to Sparkford. Brian Lugg, Alec Rollo and Mike Yorke had now left the company while Jim Scott had joined in the capacity of Production

A Sulby binder is lifted up to the first floor of the Goldcroft building during the installation of the second printing line there.

The Programatic guillotine in action at Goldcroft during January 1979. The operator is John Brooks.

The new Heidelberg 102ZP two-colour press that was installed at Goldcroft in December 1979. Kevin Brown checks the print quality.

Manager during June 1978, with Roger Stagg now as his assistant. The day-to-day running of the print room at Goldcroft was in the hands of Pete Vallis, who had been with the company since December 1972 and had responsibility for the colour printing when it was at Ilchester.

Some of the room taken up by the Editorial Department on its return to Sparkford had become available when the Sales Department moved next door into Home Farm. In February 1978 Tim Parker left to join another publisher in London and Jeff Clew was appointed Managing Editor. Further changes in the department occurred during December 1978, when Jeff became the company's first Editorial Director and Rod Grainger was appointed Managing Editor of G. T. Foulis, Pete Ward becoming the Car Workshop Manuals Editor. Soon, the Editorial Department moved into Home Farm. Pete Ward was appointed to the Board as an Editorial Director on 1 June 1983, soon after Robin Wager, who had joined the Board as an Editorial Director, had left after acquiring the Volkswagen magazine *Safer Motoring* for which he had worked previously as Assistant Editor. By this time Jeff Clew's title had been changed to that of Executive Editorial Director.

The Sales Department was another that had seen many changes. When John Hall left Sparkford to settle in California, he was succeeded by Geoff Cowen, whose main responsibility was selling to the book trade. In due course he took on the additional responsibility of sales for both J. H. Haynes & Co Ltd and G. T. Foulis, which included control of the motor trade freelance agents. When he left, he was replaced by Terry Egan, a Scotsman who had worked for John Bartholomew & Son Ltd, the map publishers of Edinburgh. Terry took up office in May 1976 and soon made his mark, being responsible for reshaping the department. One of his first moves was to recruit Andy Lynch as his assistant in November that year. Andy had the ideal background and experience, having worked for Albion Scott, a wholesale motor book distributor. Two other Albion Scott employees joined at more or less the same time, Bob Alexander in October and Phil Dennis in December, and became the nucleus of the company's own full-time sales force, which meant that the services of most of the freelance agents could be terminated. Two of the freelance agents were retained as they recognised the potential growth and had themselves taken on additional staff so that their efforts could be increased.

Terry Egan became the company's Marketing Director in November 1977, and Andy Lynch was promoted to Marketing Manager. The motor accessory trade was then going through a period of change, with the opening of cash-and-carry warehouses. The sales force was increased accordingly and sales aids such as display stands, banners and special sales campaigns became the order of the day. Before long the slogan 'Haynes Manuals Explain Best' began to appear on header boards and even on the cardboard boxes in which the books were packed. Business expanded so rapidly that this and the ever-increasing output meant that many of the larger stockists were no longer able to check their stock so were often unaware they had sold out of certain titles.

As a result, a team of merchandisers was recruited, usually ladies employed on a part-time basis, to carry out regular stock checks on a customer's premises and advise him what and when to order.

When Terry Egan left during the autumn of 1979, Andy Lynch continued to run the department and was appointed Sales and Marketing Director on 1 June 1980. Although much of the reshaping of the department had taken place whilst it was located in Home Farm, expansion decreed a move to Ilchester where room was available for setting up a training school for merchandisers and the broadening of marketing activities with storage space available for display material.

Back at Sparkford the not inconsiderable task of planning, erecting and fitting out the new Print Room extension was receiving full attention. After the plans had been drawn up by MGH Associates and planning permission had been granted, the old farmyard site was cleared and levelled, the drains were put in and the concrete poured, so that the erection of the structural steelwork could proceed. By the end of 1980 not only had all the printing equipment been moved in from Goldcroft and become fully operational but also a third Harris web offset press had been installed to complement the original press purchased in 1977 and another that was added soon afterwards, both presses having been moved from the old factory. Heavily involved with movement and re-installation of equipment was another long-serving employee, Alan Howden, who had joined the company in November 1972. Alan was responsible for the maintenance and upkeep of the company's plant and equipment, aided by electrician Terry Philips. To cope with the anticipated increase in output, the typesetting facilities had been upgraded and computerised, the keyboards now being linked to visual display units and

Extensive demolition of the buildings surrounding the old yard at Home Farm proved necessary when the decision was made to extend the Sparkford Print Room and consolidate all activities on the one site.

The outbuildings were mostly stables and one large wooden hut. The old mounting block and pump were preserved and left in their original positions.

Erection of the structural steelwork by MGH Associates soon provided ample evidence of the vast area the new Print Room extension would occupy.

information stored on rigid discs, dispensing with the need for punched tape.

The official opening of the new extension took place on 9 January 1981 when the Rt Hon Robert Boscawen, the local Member of Parliament, performed the opening ceremony, with the Vicar of Sparkford, the Reverend Patrick Connor, and representatives from Yeovil Council, the Parish Council and other civic dignitaries in attendance. Jim Scott played a major role in supervising the entire Print Room extension project, which had become one of his responsibilities following his appointment to the Board as Works Director in October 1979.

With production once again consolidated on the Sparkford site, attention could be given to the planning of a new Southern Area warehouse, in the place occupied by the old, red-painted, Dutch barn. Plans were approved by the local planning authority and work was just about to commence with the demolition of the barn when fate once again took a hand.

During the night of Friday, 25 July 1980, the barn caught fire under mysterious circumstances. Part of the report in the local newspaper, the *Western Gazette*, read as follows: 'It was well alight when the three appliances from Castle Cary reached the scene at 11pm. There was danger that the

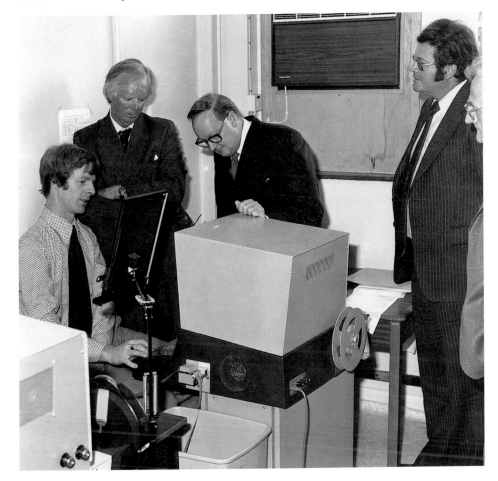

The local Member of Parliament, the Rt Hon Robert Boscawen MC, MP, always had a great interest in the company and its activities. He made early arrangements for a complete tour of the premises soon after the Conservative party was returned to power in 1979. Here, Paul Young explains the then-new photo-typesetting installation.

electric cables serving the factory would catch light, but the fire was brought under control by the 20 firemen after two hours. They were still dousing the tons of smouldering waste paper and cardboard eleven hours later. Mr Scott said the barn was completely destroyed but the fire did not spread to the neighbouring factory. It was used to store 5cwt bales of waste paper, 15,000 packing cartons and a large number of display stands'. The possibility of arson could not be ruled out, especially as two previous unsuccessful attempts had been discovered at an earlier date, elsewhere on the site. It brought home the need for a really good security arrangement when the premises were locked up for the night or at weekends, and immediate steps were taken to ensure the site would be much more secure than it had been in the past.

Like the new Print Room extension, the 14,000 square foot Southern Area Distribution warehouse was purpose-built, making maximum use of the height to give the greatest possible volume for a sophisticated side-loading fork lift racking installation. The building was completed on schedule, the stock of 400,000 books being moved by three lorries running virtually non-stop between Goldcroft and Sparkford over a weekend in November 1983. The warehouse had moved back to Goldcroft after the printing operation had

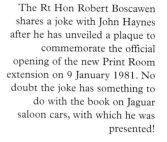

The Rt Hon Robert Boscawen shares a joke with John Haynes after he has unveiled a plaque to commemorate the official opening of the new Print Room extension on 9 January 1981. No doubt the joke has something to do with the book on Jaguar saloon cars, with which he was presented!

The gathering machine had a total of 24 stations so that even a very large manual could be completed in one pass – which was not possible with the older equipment it replaced.

Inside the new Print Room extension which was opened in 1981, showing the three Harris web offset presses needed to keep pace with the ever-increasing demand for *Owners Workshop Manuals.*

been transferred to the new extension at Sparkford so that the Park Road premises could be let after all its occupants had moved out. Betty Hill was due to retire by the time the new warehouse came into operation and Ron Tucker succeeded her as Distribution Manager. The Park Road building was converted by its new tenant into a most successful night club known as 'The Gardens' at which the company later held its annual dinner and dance. It was very hard to recall the old neat piled rows of books then replaced by the lush green vegetation and realistic palm trees that became so much a popular feature.

Mention has yet to be made of the canteen, which started initially at Camway House when Annette Haynes began cooking for three or four apprentices. Soon she was feeding 12–13 people a day at lunchtime, so when the move to Sparkford took place, a professional chef was taken on. The new

The day after the disastrous fire in the old Dutch barn. The fire destroyed all the cardboard boxes in which books were packed prior to despatch. Local firemen are pictured still damping down the smouldering remains.

Plenty of smoke, but fortunately no longer any fire. Another view of the sad aftermath.

canteen soon outgrew its original location and moved to the ground floor of Home Farm, after its acquisition and refurbishment. Its popularity grew and when even more room was needed it was transferred to one of the reconstructed outbuildings. Ably managed by Lynn House, with her staff of very efficient ladies, it provided good value for money, with a subsidy from the company to keep prices at a reasonable level. A separate room was available in which the Directors could entertain visitors, with an identical menu. John Haynes was known to startle one or two high-powered city gentlemen used to dining at the Savoy or the Ritz by announcing that they would be lunching in the canteen during their visit!

On 15 July 1981 the company celebrated its 21st Anniversary with an 'Open Day' to which customers, authors, the Press and local dignitaries were invited. They were entertained to a buffet lunch in a marquee erected on the front lawn of Home Farm and by helicopter flights as well as various competitions in which they could participate. The day opened with a bang in the literal sense of the word when three attractive promotion girls positioned themselves in front of the main building to make sure no one parked in the forecourt. Opposite is a road leading off to the right, and as luck would have it, the girls walked out to take up their positions just as a car stopped to turn

This aerial view shows the rebuilt 'piggeries' warehouse in the right foreground, and the completed Print Room extension in the background. The empty car park provided a landing space for the helicopter from which this photograph was taken, this being the day of the company's 21st Anniversary celebrations.

right. Clad in very short and tight skirts, they provided a source of distraction, so that the inevitable happened. A following car ran into the back of the one that had stopped, a second car followed suit, then a third and eventually a fourth! Fortunately no one was hurt and the damage to each car was slight, but by now the girls were behind the low wall of the forecourt protesting their innocence to a policeman!

After 13 hectic and exciting years, Frank Day sought early retirement and left the company on 31 May 1984 to let someone younger step into his shoes. It was a moving occasion to see someone with such long service depart, and the generosity of those who contributed to his leaving present was a measure of their respect for him. He was succeeded by Jim Scott, who had been appointed Deputy Managing Director in October 1980. Being generally a young company as regards the average age of its employees, retirements were relatively uncommon. The distinction of being the first had gone to Mrs Ellen Mead of the Bindery, and another who deserves mention in this context was the ever-cheerful Len Garland who, as General Assistant, possessed an amazing amount of energy that would shame many half his age. Sadly, his retirement was not the happy occasion it should have been, following the death of his wife after a long illness. Sparkford later mourned the loss of David Stead and Bruce Gilmour, both car manual authors, Dennis Lowe, who was in charge of the Bindery, and Berni Meyrick, who was a Bindery Assistant, while more recently, the sudden death of Berni Goldrick, the reader and

Sydney Harding, Mayor of Yeovil, replies to John Haynes's welcoming address at the company's 21st Anniversary buffet luncheon in Sparkford on 15 July 1981.

A luncheon group comprising (left to right): Ken Widdowson and Martyn Sharpe (Maccess), George Magnus and the late Graham Wade (Wade Marketing), and John Haynes.

Retirements were rare in the early days of the company, but Len Garland seems to be making the most of his big day as Jim Scott prepares to present him with his leaving gifts.

proof-checker, came as a great shock in late 1999. In California, tragedy struck at the office staff with Bette Stulle, in many ways the US equivalent of Frank Day, falling victim to cancer in 1978. Subsequently Helen Logreco and Betty Miller also died of cancer. In a relatively small company losses such as these are felt all the more.

So many moves of personnel and departments had taken place during the past decade, albeit for very necessary reasons at the time, that those involved regarded it as an occupational hazard described by some as 'Pickford's disease'. One unit continued to work from an outlying site: the Research Workshop, in which vehicles were stripped and rebuilt for the origination of the workshop manuals, remained at the Bennetts Field Industrial Estate in Wincanton until it was possible to accommodate it in the front of the main building at Sparkford, where at one time the stand-by electricity generator had been housed. The photographic facility had also been moved to Wincanton at the same time as the workshop. It was moved there in

The only satisfactory answer for improved management accommodation was to build a second storey on the front of the Sparkford building. This scenic view shows the preparatory work in progress.

June 1981 so that the paste-up and layout studio could be relocated in the downstairs area at the rear of the main building at Sparkford, where the workshop had been since 1972. The extra space upstairs was put to good use by the keyboard operators and the typesetting system, and was later added to by the building of an executive suite on the roof of the single storey part of the main building that fronted on to the A303. By relocating the workshop and photographic facility to Wincanton, the servicing and repair of all the company-owned vehicles could be undertaken there too.

The Research Workshop had also seen many changes since Brian Horsfall stripped and rebuilt his first project vehicle – a Reliant Regal three-wheeler – on a pile of pallets in the garage that adjoined John Haynes's home in West Camel. Brian, who had joined the company in January 1972, was another of the long-serving employees, and was Workshop and Transport Manager, aided by two fully trained mechanics. The photographic side was handled by Les Brazier, who had graduated at Queens University, Belfast and then saw service in the Fleet Air Arm. He had also joined the company in 1972 and had an assistant to help him. Every workshop manual necessitated the photographer working in conjunction with a trained mechanic, under the direction of the author originating the manual's text. This concept has been

The completed suite of offices not only provided much-needed accommodation but also improved the outside appearance of the building.

Early in 1985, a new five-colour
Heidelberg press was purchased
at a cost of approximately
£500,000. It was shipped from
Germany in sections, to be
reassembled on site. One of the
units is shown being man-
handled into position.

A special gantry was erected
within the Sparkford Print Room
extension to aid assembly of the
individual colour units and to
permit their movement into
position. Two of the installation
crew discuss the next move.

responsible for the unparalleled success of Haynes manuals and has been modified only in more recent years to take advantage of advances in modern technology, as explained later.

David Haynes, by now a Chartered Secretary, rejoined the company on 1 October 1979 in a part-time capacity as Assistant Company Secretary prior to leaving the RAF in 1981 when Mr Harold Haynes senior could hand over to him the role of Company Secretary. David Haynes also replaced David Suter as Finance Director on 1 June 1981, a post he had filled on a part-time basis for the two previous years.

Two further appointments to the Main Board followed. David Quayle was elected a Non-Executive Director on 1 January 1983, bringing with him a strong background of marketing as the founder and former Chairman of B&Q (Retail) Ltd DIY Supercentres. Subsequent appointments included that of Roger Stagg to Production Director on 1 June 1983, with Simon Slade becoming Production Manager. On the production side, Pete Vallis was promoted to Bindery and Print Room Manager. On 26 October 1984 Max Pearce joined the Main Board, also as a Non-Executive Director. He too had a distinguished marketing career with companies in the Burmah-Castrol group, having founded Maccess in 1974, the country's largest automotive trade cash-and-carry business.

Jeff Clew presents a company cheque to Mr D. Cluett, Chairman of the Sparkford Parish Council, to enable additional street lights to be placed in Church Road, Sparkford, with Mr H. Bishop, a Council member, right. The Haynes Publishing Group has always taken a keen interest in local community affairs.

5

Sparkford, Los Angeles and where?

During June 1975, after the company had been set up in the USA in 1974, it was decided to ship to Britain the 5½-litre Ford Econoline van that had been purchased by Haynes Publications Inc. It had become redundant because it had been found more economic and efficient to use local trucking companies, who would call daily to pick up boxes of books and deliver them not only within the Los Angeles basin, but to other American and Canadian cities some thousands of miles away.

There was ample evidence of need for a Ford Econoline *Owners Workshop Manual*, as by this time all manner of variants of this vehicle had become a familiar sight on the American highways. More and more emphasis was being placed on the need for titles on US domestic cars and light commercial vehicles in the USA, and with no known example of the Econoline available in Britain, the imported example could be stripped down and rebuilt in the Sparkford workshop to form the basis of the manual. Also,

The Ford Econoline van which gave rise to a local joke concerning the whereabouts of Leeds. Painted red, and with white lettering, it proved quite distinctive and a mobile source of publicity. Capable of high speeds, it was instantly recognisable by the police too!

it was considered that the appearance of such an uncommon vehicle in Britain would carry with it a certain amount of prestige, especially if it were to be repainted in the company's livery and appropriately sign written.

When the workshop session had been completed and windows had been fitted in the body to help offset the disadvantages of left-hand drive, the Econoline soon became a familiar sight on the roads of Somerset and the adjoining counties, painted bright red and with the words, 'Leeds, Sparkford and Los Angeles' in white along both sides and across the rear doors. Soon it ventured further afield, for the massive V8 engine, which would provide acceleration from 0 to 60mph in about eight seconds, made it ideally suited for 'wanted yesterday' deliveries in the South and South West. Power steering and automatic transmission made the driver's role much easier when covering long distances and, capable of carrying a 2½-ton payload, the van could reach its destination well in advance of normal schedules, whilst keeping on the right side of the law – if only just!

The place names painted on the van soon gave rise to a story that is still quoted today. It concerns one of the locals who, when talking to John Haynes one evening happened to say, 'I know where Sparkford be 'cos I live there, and I know all about Los Angeles because I've see'd it on my tele. But where be Leeds?' If not entirely true, it shows the impact the van had locally, not everyone being aware that Haynes Publications Inc was already well-established in California, and growing fast.

As far as Leeds was concerned, the original warehouse there had been acquired during July 1973, to provide better and more frequent deliveries to customers in the north of England and Scotland. Known as Globe Mills, the

The first warehouse in Leeds, shortly after refurbishing. It was opened in September 1973 but gave rise to problems on account of the deadweight of books stored.

12,000 square foot four-storey building in Globe Road had been a tobacco warehouse and, being close to the centre of Leeds, it was only about five minutes from the M1 and M62 motorways, at the heart of the motorway network. It backed on to a canal and had a deep, walled frontage which made it ideal for parking lorries. Movement of stock into the building commenced during September, involving the transfer of something like 80 tons of books from the Despatch Department at Sparkford. It had not been without its problems either, for although special racking had been put up to contain the 110 different titles that constituted the range of manuals at that time, the manner in which the pallets were arranged proved critical. The stout wooden floors began to sag ominously in some areas, due to the uneven weight distribution, so that a builder had to be called in rapidly to build brick piers under the middle of the joists that were bowing the most. Amusingly, when the warehouse was vacated some years later, the joists sprung back up again, leaving a gap of 3–4 inches between the underneath of the joists and the top of the brick pillars! Even at the best of times the warehouse looked as though it was in imminent danger of toppling over into the canal without warning, an impression not helped by the tendency for the base of the lift shaft to fill with water on the odd occasion. But it served its new purpose well and was in full operation by the end of September.

Initially, David Richards, formerly manager of the Sparkford Despatch Department, was appointed to run it, and a company house was purchased for him in Leeds. Although he was diligent and hard-working, the extra responsibility and difficulty of working so far from the Sparkford base, where so many back-up facilities were on hand, showed it would be better for him to return to Sparkford where the Despatch Department was now being run by the ever-cheerful and industrious Betty Hill. He was succeeded by Ron Encell, who had joined the company in September 1975 from National Panasonic, where he had been a warehouse manager. Being a straightforward, blunt-speaking Yorkshireman, he soon had the Leeds warehouse in good shape.

The occupants of the Leeds warehouse often used to gaze wistfully across the road at an enormous and more modern warehouse that had been empty for some time. There were large 'for lease' signs on the building, but because it had always been company policy to buy outright whenever possible in order to preserve cash flow, there seemed no chance of being able to move in. Yet at the very time when Globe Mills had become desperately short of space, the lease signs disappeared and were replaced by 'for sale' notices. Frank Day and John Haynes lost no time in making their bid and within a few weeks contracts had been exchanged and the freehold of the building purchased for £200,000. Built in the late 1950s, the building was strongly constructed being designed to house heavy, battery-driven milk floats and had an internal road (complete with traffic light!) that led to the first floor. The 32,500 square feet at first floor level, nearly three times the area of the old warehouse, proved more than adequate, so the ground floor was let to a

John Haynes explains the finer details of his TVR Tuscan sprint racing car to guest of honour, Tony Lanfranchi, at the opening of the new Leeds warehouse on 21 November 1979. Frank Day is on the far left, and Ron Encell on the right.

tenant. A further 45,000 square feet were allocated for redevelopment. Previously owned by the Leeds Co-operative Society, the new property provided not only the much-needed extra space but also allowed for future expansion.

Before the end of 1979 the new warehouse, known as Globe Works, was in full operation. At an official opening ceremony on 21 November, Tony Lanfranchi, a well-known driver in northern racing circles, was invited as guest of honour. John Haynes had never been able to finish anywhere near him when they raced together at circuits such as Rufforth, so as a Yorkshireman it seemed most appropriate to have him perform the opening ceremony.

Customers attending the opening ceremony had the opportunity to view a small but interesting collection of vehicles that comprised a 6.6-litre Ford Country Esquire Estate, a much-modified TVR Tuscan sprint racing car, a 1929 dirt track Velocette motorcycle reputed to be the sole survivor of only 22 made, and a Honda ATC 110 'fun' three-wheeler. The last was one of the first ATCs to be imported into Britain, arriving before Honda (UK) Ltd's own shipment. Like the Ford Econoline and the Country Squire Estate, it had been shipped from California, for yet another workshop manual project intended for the US market.

Before the guests began to arrive, some of the Haynes directors sought to amuse themselves by trying to navigate the Honda ATC around a cleared area of the warehouse. Having no differential on its rear wheels, the Honda showed a marked inclination not to deviate from a straight line, even when the handlebars were turned, until the rider appreciated the need to lift one of the rear wheels. Piled boxes of books proved very hard on the kneecaps when run into, one or two of the directors developing a noticeable limp after such encounters! Andy Lynch proved the most proficient in handling the ATC and could even pull a wheelie or two!

6

The US operation

It was always known that the North American market was one of tremendous importance; it had a car 'parc' of over 150 million vehicles and between 8 and 10 million new cars were being sold each year. It was a market that John Haynes knew he would need to break into if the workshop manual side of the business was to expand significantly. By the early 1970s there were sufficient numbers of cars being imported from Europe and Japan that were already covered by a Haynes Manual to justify an attempt. The manuals would require only superficial modification to make them suitable for the American market, mainly with regard to left-hand drive, carburation details and lighting equipment in the case of cars, and only the last in the case of motorcycles.

Admittedly the problems became more acute as time progressed, when strict emission controls were imposed in an attempt to reduce atmospheric pollution, but when the decision to go in was taken, they were of less significance.

An early attempt to break into the American market was made during 1971, through co-operation with a New York publisher, Drake Publishing. Rather than have them sell Haynes Manuals in their UK format, it was agreed the books would be printed with a special cover of Drake's own design that would embody their logo. It seemed a very promising proposition and over a two-year period a large number of manuals were shipped out with their new covers. But as time went by, the orders from Drake increased in size whilst their payments got slower and slower, until eventually it was decided they could no longer be supplied because the Government's Export Credit Guarantee (ECGD) limit of $50,000 had been reached. Fortunately, under the ECGD scheme, the Government had guaranteed a 90 per cent refund of the financial outlay if the deal went wrong and, had it not been for this undertaking, the company would have found itself standing a substantial loss.

In 1973, an approach was made by Walt Haessner, of Haessner Publishing Inc in New Jersey, who had a number of motoring books on his list and was confident he could sell Haynes Manuals. As a result, he was supplied with them in their standard UK cover, by means of an 'on consignment' basis, so that he only paid for stock when he had sold it. After six months or so, it became quite apparent that although Walt was a charming man, a great motoring enthusiast, and very good company, he was not selling the stock in the quantity expected. So after two false starts it was considered that the best thing to do would be to go back to first principles and set up an associate business in America, warehousing and marketing the manuals through the company's own US outlet. Although there was no chance of getting an ECGD for a venture of this nature, and the risk of failure was obviously high, all the directors agreed upon this course of action.

The decision to locate in Los Angeles was taken not only because the Japanese importers had their headquarters on the West Coast and the latest and most up-to-date models were shipped there, but also because California itself was an enormous market containing some 24,000,000 cars and was renowned for the enthusiasm of its automobile and motorcycle buffs. (The fact that California is noted for its superb climate, pretty girls, cheap food and drink and proximity to the Pacific Ocean, had nothing to do with it, we're told!)

The first two months of 1974 saw much activity in writing to property firms, lawyers and accountants in Los Angeles, with a view to doing all the preparatory work before flying out there. At the beginning of April, John Haynes and John Hall flew to New York where, over a splendid meal at La Chanteclair, run by the Dreyfus brothers, it was agreed quite amicably with Walt Haessner that he would stop selling Haynes Manuals and, as soon as the new company was established in California, he would ship what stock he had left to them to begin selling. René Dreyfus had been a racing driver of great distinction and a former champion driver of France, so the meeting place was one that greatly befitted the occasion.

Two weeks of feverish activity followed, during which time much credit must go to David Morgan, a partner at American law firm Voeglin & Barton who, from John Haynes's first enquiry from the UK, had been very much on the ball, having replied to the initial letter by return. He turned out to be very much an Anglophile, and with his help Haynes Publications Inc was formed on 24 April 1974 with 500,000 authorised shares at no par value, 1,000 of them being duly issued. It was with great pleasure that the following telex was received from Frank Day, immediately after the company was formed. It read: 'To Mr J. H. Haynes, Statler Hilton, Wilshire Boulevard, Los Angeles, California. Congratulations on setting up subsidiary company Haynes Publications Inc. Should be available to meet your anticipated heavy demands. Best wishes, Head Office.' At such a time, it was very much appreciated.

Barry Piggott was taken on as Vice-President and General Manager to run the American operation, and commission agents Cohn & Shane were appointed to sell the books. Bud Cohn, in his late 70s, had a splendid collection of motor cars which, after his death some ten years later, were sold at auction, where his Mercedes-Benz 500K White Roadster fetched the then-record price of $405,000. A Ford Econoline van was purchased to make deliveries and 1,750 square feet of warehousing with office accommodation in front was rented at 9421, Winnetka Avenue, Chatsworth. Located in the San Fernando Valley, to the north-west of downtown Los Angeles, the warehouse was not far from the foothills of the Santa Susana mountains.

Barry, an expatriate Englishman, had been working with a firm of Mazda importers in California and had helped with the production of the Haynes Mazda RX2 manual in March 1973. One of his first moves was to take on a very competent book-keeper, Bette Stulle, whose tough and uncompromising attitude helped ensure the cash rolled in quickly when the books were sold, and whose business philosophy was very similar to that of Frank Day. After she had met Frank, a few years later, she always kept a bottle of his favourite Scotch at her home for whenever he might visit. But even her skills could not help the company in those first six months. The accountants had worked out that 7,000 manuals had to be sold each month just to break even and the company was a long way off its target, so inevitably the UK company had to support it. California was visited several times that year, and it is interesting to recall the monthly fixed expenses that were being incurred, those of July 1974 being typical:

Telephone	$70.00
Salaries and wages	$2,680.00
FICA	$120.00
+ 3.6 per cent, of $2,680.00	
Stationery	$50.00
Telex	$200.00
Water cooler	$12.00
Trash pick-up	$14.00
Truck/gasoline/maintenance	$100.00
B. Piggott's expenses	$50.00
Postage	$150.00
R. Coulton landlord rent	$264.45
Gas/water/electricity	$30.00
Packing material	$75.00

In addition to this were variable costs, such as incoming freight, outgoing freight, commission to agents, the cost of display racks, and other small incidental expenses.

Throughout this period there was rock-hard determination on the part of all those concerned to ensure that the business would eventually become successful and everything possible was being done to make this happen. All the publicity and advertising material was Americanised, and it was a period of considerable learning, for it was recognised that to sell successfully in America one had to take on the appearance of being American.

It soon became obvious that Barry was not the super-salesman he needed to be to get the embryonic company off the ground, and after much discussion, John Hall agreed to take on the role. John had done an excellent job in England in lining up the freelance commission agents and getting the manuals into non-bookshop and accessory shop outlets, and he welcomed the challenge that the USA and Canada would present, as well as appreciating that here was a once-in-a-lifetime opportunity not to be missed. So, on 29 September 1974 John and Angie Hall flew out to Los Angeles to take up permanent residence there. Fortunately, Barry Piggott had been offered his job back with his old company, so the hand-over was quite amicable and Haynes Publications Inc was now set fair on its new course.

Haynes did not, however, have the market to themselves, particularly as Clymer Publications was also located in the Greater Los Angeles area and had a similar interest in car and motorcycle workshop manuals. Having been in the business a great deal longer, Clymer resented the intrusion of a newcomer, particularly one from outside the USA. In consequence, a strong sense of rivalry developed, which grew more intense as Haynes Manuals began to make serious inroads into their sales. To strengthen Haynes's market share, an attempt was made in 1977 to produce manuals on US domestic cars by bringing across Brian Horsfall (who was then in charge of the Sparkford

Before the US operation got under way, US domestic cars were borrowed from American servicemen stationed in the UK and stripped and rebuilt at Sparkford. Martin Penny lifts the engine from a Chevrolet Nova as the first stage in the manual destined for the American market.

workshop) and Les Brazier (the Sparkford photographer) to work at Winnetka Avenue for a month, stripping and rebuilding cars and recording the entire project on tape and film. But the facilities available proved to be too primitive and the project was abandoned until such time as a more permanent arrangement could be made. As a stopgap, American cars were borrowed from US airbases in England on a loan-cum-repair basis, stripped and rebuilt at Sparkford, and the finished books sent to America. Not only was it then cheaper to print in England and ship the manuals to America in containers at regular intervals, but in addition it created extra print work for Sparkford and therefore helped to increase profitability.

Due to the vastness of the country, sales initially were concentrated in California which, in itself, is about the size of the United Kingdom. Use was made of commission agents in much the same way as in England, but marketing methods were quite different because there was not the correspondingly large number of motor accessory shops, a large proportion of business being handled by mail order. Appearances at trade shows, exhibitions and dealer displays helped bring the Haynes name to the fore, especially as none of the competitors based their manuals on the complete stripdown and rebuild of a vehicle, and Haynes Publications Inc made this a strong selling point. Gradually trade increased, and the company was helped by the country itself getting into the DIY era, simply because America too was facing a recession with a rising rate of inflation. No longer was it possible to take an ailing vehicle to a repairer with the terse instruction to 'fix it'.

It was soon obvious that a larger warehouse would be required if growth along its present lines continued, so when the warehouse next door became empty, the company snapped up the extra 3,000 square feet of space. By the spring of 1975, Haynes Publications Inc was making a profit and books were being produced specifically for the American market. John and Annette Haynes visited America four or five times during the year and by the end of 1975 there were 67 automotive repair and tune-up manuals on the American market, together with 30 motorcycle manuals, all bearing the Haynes imprint. Now that the American company was trading profitably, it was time to expand into North America as a whole, so in the spring of 1976 John and Annette purchased a house in Westhills, just outside West Los Angeles and a few miles from the Ventura Freeway, with the intention later in the year of spending at least 12 months in America helping John Hall to get the business really moving. They left for Westhills on 13 September that year with their youngest son, Christopher. Reluctantly, JJ and Marc, the two elder boys, had to be left behind as they were well established in their UK boarding schools. With the family so split up, many trips were taken in 1977/78 to attend half terms and to take the children to the USA for their holidays. Sometimes the boys travelled alone, which they enjoyed very much as the female cabin crew were very kind and attentive, quite spoiling them! When Christopher was four years old he enjoyed his first visit to Las Vegas, but not to gamble – John and Annette were attending the APAA trade show.

Two weeks after arriving in Los Angeles, and having taken up residence in Vickiview Drive in Westhills, Helen Logreco, who looked after various customers and their accounts, went on holiday while Annette stalwartly took on her position. This was much to the amusement of one customer who, on hearing a strange English voice at the end of the telephone, queried who was speaking, and after Annette's reply, said humorously, 'Gee, must be the boss's wife, I guess they will employ anyone there'!

In 1977, with sales benefiting from the attention of the two Johns, it became obvious that Haynes Publications Inc was once again rapidly running out of warehouse space, so a search was started to find a suitable replacement for Winnetka Avenue. After viewing a couple of dozen or so buildings, a suitable property was found in a much more rural area just outside the county limits of Los Angeles, at Newbury Park in the county of Ventura. Travelling to work would be much easier as it would be against the rush-hour traffic, and it was a much more pleasant area in which to work, being not far from Thousand Oaks and Westlake Village, as well as the Pacific coastline. In May 1977, 861, Lawrence Drive became the new address, with a larger 11,000 square foot warehouse and improved office accommodation. The off ramp was sign-posted Rancho Conejo and indeed, the business increased just like rabbits over the next two years. It was at this time that Jeff Shifman joined the company to help with sales and marketing.

The move took place over two days in the middle of August, some 38,000 books being moved on pallets by two hired lorries. The throttle on one of them jammed open and the warehouseman driving it had the fright of his life when he also found that he was being chased by a police car with its lights flashing and siren screaming. Eventually he managed to stop the vehicle, and with the help of the police, sorted out the problem. He was so obviously badly shaken by this incident that the police proffered no charges at all, which for Southern California, where speeding tickets are mandatory, was most unusual!

A change occurred when John Hall left to work on his own for a brief period as a commission representative, handling products for other people. He then joined Ernest and Warren Hartley, two brothers who originally came from Lancashire and ran a large and prosperous automotive warehouse distribution business just outside San Diego. The company's name was Kingsbourne, and it was then one of the more important US accounts, John being able to use his in-depth knowledge of the Haynes product line to great advantage when dealing with Kingsbourne's customers. His place was taken by Pete O'Donohue, another English expatriate who was already working in the USA and who had experience of the car accessory trade. He joined Haynes Publications Inc in September 1977 to take over the reins and play a leading role in the continuing expansion of sales.

It was during 1978 that Clymer Publications Inc, the company's main competitor, filed an anti-dumping petition with the US Treasury against the Haynes Publishing Group, now that they were faced with really aggressive competition that had taken 25 per cent of their business right on their own doorstep. They saw this as a means of attempting to offset their lost sales because, if the case could be substantiated, a discriminatory tax could be levied against all Haynes Manuals imported into the USA which would effectively shut the door completely. The investigation that followed presented a very busy and worrying time for John Haynes, who had to make several trips to Washington in the summer, to give evidence before the Federal authorities in court. But at the end of the day, the General Council of the Treasury Department signed an order terminating the investigation, its two commissioners having decided that Clymer had failed to establish even a reasonable indication of injury under the Anti-Dumping Act. The biter had been bit, and no time was lost in putting out a press release headed 'Clymer climbs down'. But at the same time, a profound feeling of respect developed for a country that was big enough and honest enough to allow free commercial competition within its frontiers from other free countries in the world.

It is interesting, and perhaps amusing, to note that the increased output of manuals in the UK, many of which were shipped to the USA, had been achieved by using newly installed equipment of American origin! This included the photo-typesetting equipment made by Dymo Graphic Systems, of Wilmington, Massachusetts and web offset printing presses made by the Harris Intertype Corporation, of Fort Worth, Texas!

The need for manuals about US domestic cars and light commercial vehicles became more and more pressing, particularly when the need for fuel conservation brought about the birth of the American-made 'compact' car of the late 1970s. There was only one long-term answer – to set up in Newbury Park an editorial team parallel to that operating at Sparkford, so that with matching workshop facilities, an identical stripdown and rebuild procedure could be followed. After recruitment of staff by Terry Grimwood, who was an experienced editor from the UK who set up the US editorial team, this came into being during 1978. Initially they sent their manuscripts to Sparkford for typesetting and printing, but later undertook the typesetting and layout work themselves. The extra room needed was found quite conveniently in March that year when the warehouse next door at 859 Lawrence Drive became available, adding an additional 11,000 square feet. As a result, there was then a total of 22,000 square feet of modern warehousing and offices available at Newbury Park.

After one year as Managing Editor, Terry Grimwood returned to the UK as his family was unable to settle in California and his wife, in particular, missed England and their many close relatives. Scott Mauck was then promoted to this position and soon became a Vice President, a post which he has held with skill and much competence to this day. He celebrated 20 years with the Group in November 1999, a truly fine achievement especially when popular myth will have it that Californians move jobs and houses every three years or so!

The manuals originated at Newbury Park are directed mainly at the US market, although instances have occurred where the Newbury Park and Sparkford editorial departments have worked in close co-operation to produce manuals that are suitable for both markets and also to update existing titles. Fortunately, the US-destined manuals were always easy to identify as they had soft covers, there being no demand for hard covers as is the case with the UK market.

Printing was carried out at Sparkford for all manuals and there was a regular shipment of finished books by 40ft long containers, each holding about 30,000 copies. This part of the operation was handled by Colin Hughes, Sparkford's Purchasing Manager, under the guidance of Annette Haynes, the Co-ordinating Director who formed the vital link between the US and UK companies. She also set the reprint programme to ensure all titles were always in stock. Gone were the days in the late 1970s when demand had been so heavy that it was usual to have 20 to 30 titles out of stock. Even one title out of stock these days calls for an immediate explanation!

Up to this point, Haynes Publishing Inc had been concentrating all its efforts on the automobile and motorcycle accessory aftermarkets and understandably were weak when it came to the traditional book trade, which demands a quite different approach. Whilst this situation was being reviewed,

A vehicle being stripped and rebuilt at Newbury Park in an identical manner to that which had become a well-established routine at Sparkford. An author checks out a few details during the early stages of a new project.

Another consignment of books arrives from Sparkford by container, to be off-loaded into the Newbury Park warehouse in the late 1970s.

news was received of a distributor in California who had gone into receivership for a variety of reasons that were complicated and totally understandable. Yet the company concerned had done a good job warehousing and distributing books for the smaller English and American publishers to the whole of the US market. A particularly favourable impression had been created by Matt Gouig, who had run the business on a day-to-day basis, so arrangements were made for him to visit Pete O'Donohue at Newbury Park. Their discussion proved fruitful and led to the formation of a new company called Interbook Inc, which Matt would run from premises in San Francisco, to sell specifically to the book trade in North America. It gave Pete O'Donohue a full-time salesman who could concentrate on the traditional book trade, and results were soon apparent in the form of increased sales.

US sales had risen by 39 per cent during 1980 and were producing profits at such a satisfactory level that they masked the relatively poor performance of the UK home market. In view of the UK situation it may at first seem surprising that the decision to set up an editorial team in Newbury Park had been implemented on a much larger scale than originally envisaged. During the 1980/81 financial year, high interest rates of more than 20 per cent were encouraging the major US wholesalers to run down their own stocks, while many customers involved in the wholesaling or distribution of

automobile or motorcycle parts had to rely more heavily on bank finance. It was a matter of some disappointment that at the very time when new titles were most needed to obtain a larger share of the lucrative US market, only three manuals of US origin had been published during the year.

This setback necessitated some reorganisation of staff in the American Editorial Department, accompanied by some procedural revisions and the acquisition of new equipment. Swiftly executed, these remedial measures had the desired effect and US editorial output began to show a dramatic rise by the end of the financial year. Ten new workshop manuals were available for despatch to the UK for production in the last few months prior to the year's end, and by the end of the year eight of them had been published. The fall in the exchange rate of the pound in relation to the dollar also had a favourable effect on the Group's profitability.

Difficult trading conditions prevailed throughout the 1981/82 financial year and remained a continuing problem. In recession-hit America the automobile manufacturers were having to face up to severe financial difficulties resulting from a dramatic shortfall in sales. They had fallen even lower than when they took a downturn during the 1973 oil crisis. Despite this gloomy economic background, the American company's profitability had nearly doubled compared with its performance a year earlier. The US Editorial Department now matched its UK counterpart in size, and in the

An inside view of Pete O'Donohue's office at Newbury Park with the general office behind the window. Harold Miller is seated at the table, opposite Fran Taylor.

Scott Mauck in his office at Newbury Park. He has the overall responsibility for the manual editorial team and is the author of a number of titles on US domestic cars and light commercial vehicles.

face of fierce competition from America's well-established publishers, the addition of four new US domestic titles to the list provided the ability to win new accounts unconnected with the US-imported car and motorcycle business.

In acknowledgement of the excellent endeavours of everyone involved in the US company's activities an Employees Defined Benefit Plan and Pension Trust was introduced during the 1982/83 financial year. It would ensure all employees, when they reached the age of 65, would be able to look forward to a well-provided-for retirement assuming they had worked for the company for ten years or more and satisfied other requirements.

Max Pearce was appointed Executive Vice Chairman of Haynes Publications Inc and an Executive Director on the Group's Main Board on 23 August 1985. In September that year Eric Oakley was appointed Vice President of Sales and Marketing of the US company, with further promotion to follow on 5 November 1986 when he was appointed President of the US company to succeed Pete O'Donohue, who had left. Eric had joined the

The Haynes story in colour

An aerial view of the Sparkford premises in September 1993 – offices and print hall left, and the warehouse, right, which has since been extended considerably.

Annette Haynes, Max Pearce and John Haynes address members of staff and invited guests, to mark the occasion of the opening of the new print hall in 1990. Following a conducted tour of the newly installed printing facilities, a reception was held at the Motor Museum.
(Peter Nicholson)

With a background of all the Haynes motorcycle manuals then available, this stand attracted much attention at the 1983 Motor Cycle Show held at the National Exhibition Centre, Birmingham. The Suzuki Four shown here was counterbalanced by a fully restored BSA Bantam on the other end of the stand.

In 1984, sponsorship of the Haynes Four-Stroke Motocross Championship was in its eighth successive year, ending with a sensational and close-fought finish. Steve How (left, runner-up) and Dave Tomasik (right, winner) flank Jeff Clew and Lorna Wilds (who organised the championship) at the prize-giving ceremony.
(Graham Cox)

The exterior of Haynes Publications Inc at 861 Lawrence Drive, Newbury Park. Blue skies as usual for California in July; this photograph was taken in the early 1980s. The small trees and shrubs seen here have now grown and today obscure much of the building's frontage.

Far left: John Hall, the late Helen Logreco and two members of the Haynes Publications Inc staff outside the original Winnetka Avenue premises in 1977.

Left: John Haynes and Pete O'Donohue are interviewed for a television programme about Haynes Manuals which was screened during 1983, broadcast by the Nashville cable network to 8,000,000 viewers.

John Haynes's much modified
TVR Tuscan being put
through its paces at a
Weston-super-Mare sprint
by John Blundell.
(Nick Bradbury)

The secret of producing accurate and comprehensive manuals is to completely strip down, photograph and rebuild each vehicle. At one time, the UK Research Workshop was at Wincanton, as seen here in May 1987. In the background is the GMC Motorhome which was shipped from California and repainted in Haynes Publishing livery and has been used for exhibitions and trade days as well as the back-up vehicle for the nationwide launch tour of *The Bike Book* in 1994.

The UK Research Workshop is now at Sparkford and is a state-of-the-art facility. Here, Paul Buckland, right, uses a digital camera.

Left: The UK Motor Trade Editorial upstairs office, January 2000. Penny Cox, the Motorcycle Editorial Manager, is in the foreground.

Below left: The UK Motor Trade Editorial main office, January 2000. Note the computer-generated wiring diagram visible on Matthew Marke's screen.

Below: The Special Interest Publishing Division team, January 2000. Left to right, standing: Mark Hughes, Judy Bailey, Christine Smith, Louise McIntyre and Darryl Reach (Director). Seated, Alison Roelich and Flora Myer.

Above: The UK Production office team in January 2000, left to right: Alan Sperring (Director), Christine Adamson, Allan Bishop, Kevin Perrett, Kevin Heals and John Warry. Absent on this occasion was Andy Hayward.

Above, right: Film checking in progress at Sparkford. Left to right: Maurice Murphy, Charles Seaton, Nick Ewers and Rob Parker.

Right: The Solna web press in operation at Sparkford with Colin Goodland, left, and Dave House.

Sandra MacKinnon joined the company nearly 30 years ago and has been John Haynes's personal secretary for most of that time.

Above: The Design Department at Sparkford, January 2000 with left to right: David Hermelin and David Notley (Directors), and Simon Larkin.

Left: The picking line in the Sparkford warehouse.

Below: A UK Operations Department meeting with left to right: Maureen Wincott (Customer Services), Ian Mauger (Director), Pete Turner (Warehouse Manager), Mandy Warry and Tim Birch.

The UK Accounts
Department, February
2000, left to right, back row:
James Bunkum, Liz Clarke,
Tricia Coulson,
Colin Davies (Director).
Front: Georgina Loder,
Tami Parker, Sue White,
Dawn Davies and
Sara Belton.
(Peter Nicholson)

Maureen Wincott, left, and
the Customer Services
team, January 2000.

GROUP BOARD DIRECTORS

John Haynes, OBE

Max Pearce

Annette Haynes

David Haynes

Eric Oakley

Keith Fullman

Panton Corbett

David Suter

J. Haynes

Printing in progress at Nashville, showing the console of the Rowland 700 four-colour machine.

The Solna web in operation at Nashville.

Dan Benhardus

Don Brown

Scott Mauck

Gordon Stengel

Above: Four US Vice-Presidents. *Left*: The US Research Workshop at Newbury Park, Los Angeles.

The Haynes Publishing stand at the Frankfurt Book Fair, October 1999. Left to right: Mark Broadley and Viktoria Tischer of Overseas Development, Mark Hughes, who joined the company later in the year, and Graham Cook (Director). *(Darryl Reach)*

The Governor of Tennessee is welcomed to Sparkford to unveil the foundation stone for the Museum's extension, 4 July 1988. Left to right: John Ward (Governor's staff), not known, John Haynes, Ned McWherter, Max Pearce and Jim Scott, right.

The Scandinavian sales force about to take off from Uppsala, Sweden, February 2000, for 'some serious sales action'. Left to right: Krister Ingvarsson, Håkan Lindberg and Anders Kind.

The imposing entrance to the Haynes Motor Museum, March 2000.
(Peter Nicholson)

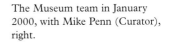

The Museum team in January 2000, with Mike Penn (Curator), right.

Christopher Haynes, Museum Development and Events Manager.

Jay Haynes arrives back at the Museum in his father's 1965 4.7-litre V8 AC Cobra during a Two-Day Classic tour in 1997. *(Peter Nicholson)*

Just part of the amazing 'Red Collection' of sports cars on display at the Haynes Motor Museum.

A general view of a small part of the Museum collection.

company in 1980 as Sales and Marketing Manager and had an Honours Degree in Economics, awarded by the University of Aston in Birmingham, England.

During 1986 steps were being taken to prepare for more growth and expansion. They would include a further expansion of the editorial facility to 4,000 square feet. Earlier that year the warehouse capacity had been doubled by installing narrow aisle racking. It was also proposed to discontinue warehousing and distribution operations for third-party publishers. Sales managers for the East Coast and the traditional book trade had already been appointed, giving rise to a further increase in expenditure in the short term with the objective of increased sales and profitability in late 1986/87.

At the end of the first half of the 1986/87 financial year the US business was losing money. However, after the management changes implemented by Max Pearce, there was a major recovery in the second half and the year was completed with record sales and profits. The commitment to switch to Haynes had been made by the growing Autozone chain (known as Auto Shack) on Christmas Eve 1986. US sales had increased by over $1 million, representing 23 per cent growth, and pre-tax trading profits were no less than 275 per cent ahead at $714,000. Substantial achievements had been made in the acquisition of new business, especially in the retail sector. The three largest automotive chain stores in the US stocked Haynes products, accounting for over 1,300 additional sales outlets. Plans were now under way to establish an additional facility in the eastern United States, to augment the existing Californian headquarters and materially improve the distribution of the Group's products in North America.

North American trading during the 1987/88 financial year proved to be

The Nashville bindery line.

John Haynes and Don Brown at the Lavergne printing, binding and distribution facility, Nashville.

Interior of the Nashville warehouse.

extremely exciting, with profits before tax up 42 per cent on the previous year. This performance would have been even more impressive had not the weakness of the dollar made its impact felt. Its effect on turnover meant the increase amounted to only 11 per cent when translated into sterling. Even so, this measure of success made it possible to bring forward the timescale of the plan for an eastern warehouse.

By the end of the 1987/88 financial year a new 36,000 square foot warehouse in Nashville, Tennessee, had been purchased for $1 million, the building and land financed entirely from the Group's own resources. In a separate negotiation on 25 July 1989 a credit line of $1.5 million was completed with the Sovran Bank to make provision for any future contingencies.

Occupying a freehold site of 4.5 acres, the Nashville warehouse became fully operational on 13 June 1988, the recruitment of key personnel having taken place during the completion of its purchase on 22 March. Investment of this nature by a British-based company was welcomed by the Governor of the State of Tennessee, Ned McWherter, who visited the Group's headquarters at Sparkford on 4 July to meet John Haynes and the other Main Board directors. Despite his busy schedule, on 10 November, Governor McWherter officially opened the Nashville warehouse.

Before the end of the year three senior appointments were made: Don Brown as Vice President of Operations in Nashville on 14 March, Bill Kilduff as Vice President of Sales on 1st September, and Dan Benhardus as Vice President of Finance on 19 October, all of whom made a significant contribution to the Group's success.

The geographical location of the eastern warehouse was critical as to have had it further north would have resulted in conditions, in winter, when transport by road would have been difficult. Nashville presented the optimum position for distribution of the Group's products to the eastern, south-eastern and mid-western states of the USA and Canada. Because despatch to three-quarters of North America could be made more easily from Nashville, rather than from California, economies would be realised in transport costs as 70 per cent of the Group's US business at that time was within a 1,000-mile radius of Nashville. All products now arrived through the eastern seaboard to Nashville, which trans-shipped to California, a three-day journey by road. The new warehouse proved extremely cost-effective and was soon distributing 80 per cent of the books sold in North America. Not only had lower distribution costs resulted but in addition it had been possible to negotiate a 25 per cent reduction in shipping charges from the UK which reflected the shorter journey to Nashville rather than that to Los Angeles.

The extremely high levels of investment required to develop new markets and to relaunch certain products suggested that it would be prudent to review the manner in which origination costs were written off as they related to products of this nature, ie, new markets and new or re-launched product lines. They could be written off over the first print run or over up to five years. This change was agreed by the Board and was implemented effective with the 1988 figures.

The US editorial team had been enlarged by the time the 1989 annual report was published, with a new, highly sophisticated typesetting computer due to be installed after the year's end. The product range was now better than that of any of the company's US publishing competitors and was being stocked by about 25 per cent of the car and motorcycle repair manual outlets.

Excellent growth continued in the USA, with an increase in turnover and a significant rise in trading profit. The acquisition of further major accounts, and a halt in the output of new automobile manuals during 1989 by Clymer, one of the company's two principal competitors, meant Haynes Publications Inc now had an increasing share of the market for car titles, which had risen from 10–15 per cent to 40 per cent after a great deal of hard work by the US sales team. The breakthrough into market dominance had been aided by strengthening this team and fully justified the expenditure on the new electronic publishing equipment.

The 1990 Annual Report confirmed excellent growth had continued with an increase of 16.8 per cent in turnover and a 41 per cent rise in trading profit. For the first time more Haynes Manuals were being sold in the USA than the UK, something John Haynes had always believed would happen. In recognition of his contribution, Eric Oakley had been appointed a director on the Group's Main Board on 22 June 1989. He and Max Pearce had been responsible for the fine results achieved in the USA.

The Annual Report for 1991 revealed just how badly the Group was hit by the recession, which struck suddenly when it was most vulnerable. As explained in Chapter 9, despite continuing growth and profitability in the

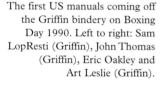

The first US manuals coming off the Griffin bindery on Boxing Day 1990. Left to right: Sam LopResti (Griffin), John Thomas (Griffin), Eric Oakley and Art Leslie (Griffin).

USA the Group effectively did no more than break even, with a profit of only £26,000 before tax compared with the 1990 figure of £3,098,000. A recovery plan was implemented and Max Pearce, who had been responsible for the successful reorganisation of the US operation to make it the most profitable part of the Group, was appointed Group Chief Executive. Part of his cost reduction and reorganisation plan included provision for manuals to be printed in the USA to take advantage of the strong sterling exchange rate in relation to the dollar. Further economies would also be realised in reduced freight charges and the lower cost of paper. Griffin Printing, who had formerly printed all of Clymer's manuals, was selected to take on this work initially. On 26 December 1990 Eric Oakley took delivery from the binders of the first manual to be printed in the USA. Griffin Printing had completed their first print run satisfactorily.

US stock holdings were reduced somewhat as a result of the shorter lead time created by the elimination of ocean freight, and further cost reductions were achieved by printing 32-page sections. Annette Haynes, who had overall control of the printing and reprinting programmes, would continue to do so initially for a six-month period. This would give the US company time to gain the necessary expertise and establish their own sales patterns so that they could ultimately make their own decisions on US print runs.

To better serve the growing North American market a new subsidiary company was formed, Haynes North America Inc to have the responsibility for the US publishing programme. Haynes Publications Inc retained the distribution business.

By the year's end good progress had been made in the USA, with a continual increase in the market share despite shark-like trading conditions. The number of new accounts, including those of some of the major retailing chains, had added to the customer base, bringing in an additional $4 million turnover. Profit, however, did not increase correspondingly. To gain new business it had been necessary to make a one-off stock uplift of competitors' product. Unfortunately the 4 per cent increase in US dollar profits translated into a small downturn in sterling due to an 11 per cent deterioration in the exchange rate.

Although poor trading conditions persisted in America and Canada throughout 1992, the US trading companies turned in a very solid performance. Profit in US dollars increased by 58 per cent, due largely to the elimination of non-recurring costs associated with the previous year and ocean freight-related savings through having the US manuals printed in the USA. By the end of the financial year the American companies were in a cash-positive situation. There was now very little transatlantic business carried out between the US and the UK companies as each served its own marketplace, using its own resources. The US Editorial Department took advantage of the situation again to upgrade its electronic publishing capabilities. By acquiring additional state-of-the-art software, greater efficiences could be achieved in the production of the US manuals.

US sales and profits were up by 9 per cent and 11 per cent respectively. This continued growth had further consolidated Haynes position as market leader throughout the USA and Canada in repair manuals specific to a particular vehicle, despite trading conditions still being very competitive. More favourable prices for raw materials, especially paper, had resulted in margins higher than anticipated. However, while white paper prices had remained lower than expected, suppliers were indicating a price rise within the next six months.

The Group established a US printing company, Odcombe Press (Nashville) Inc, on 2 July 1993. Nigel Clements was seconded from Sparkford to the US company to oversee the installation of the equipment and today is US Production Director. After installation was completed, US printing began in October that year. Initally the press ran a single shift at a production speed of 25,000 32-page sections per hour, and the bindery operations at 5,000 books per hour. Over the course of the next four years the press operations were extended to three full shifts and the bindery to two with overtime being worked on both.

The expansion of the distribution centre and print plant in Tennessee had been completed on schedule and had doubled the warehouse and office space. Again, Governor Ned McWherter in November 1993 performed the opening ceremony. It represented a significant step forward as now the Group had its own printing and book manufacturing facilities on both sides of the Atlantic with which to serve the whole of Europe and the Americas.

In July 1994, an Agfa Selectset 7000 imagesetter was added to the Nashville Pre-press Department on the understanding that Agfa would replace it with an Avantra 44 when available and this occurred in May 1995. In the

The well-equipped printing and binding facilities at Nashville include, top, this MAN Roland 700 four-colour press plus coater installed in 1998. It prints covers and cover inserts at a rate of 13,000 sheets per hour. Below, the fully automated in-line binding, shrink-wrapping cartoning and palletising operation has a capacity of producing 5,000 finished books per hour.

meantime, US business had expanded and Haynes Publications Inc – Odcombe's landlord – had found it necessary to extend the Nashville facility with the addition of 40,500 square feet of warehouse space and another 3,000 square feet of offices. Construction of the extension to the premises began in March 1995 and was completed in December the same year. At first, colour covers were not printed in-house, but in 1994 a second-hand Solna colour press was added. This was replaced in May 1997 by a state-of-the-art digital Man Roland 700 machine that is capable of producing 52,000 covers per hour.

Despite market conditions, which continued to be extremely competitive, dollar operating profits had increased by 25 per cent, which reflected the volume growth and continued production efficiencies being gained from Nashville. Although the US company had seen significant increases in the costs in raw material, management had taken steps to minimise the impact of these increases on profitability. During the latter half of the financial year the company invested in its first national television campaign.

The US business launched a line of 'task specific' manuals known as *TechBooks* at the huge Automotive Parts and Accessories Association trade show (APAA) in Las Vegas in November 1994. These were very successful, not only with existing customers but also as a 'second line' with new customers. They were subsequently added to the UK production line.

Despite poor trading in the UK during the first quarter of the 1995 financial year, the Group was still able to report an increase in pre-tax profits due to the strength of the US business. Their operating profits in sterling rose by 11 per cent and enabled Group pre-tax profits to rise by 4 per cent to £5.2 million. Work had now commenced on the addition to the warehouse and production plant in Nashville and was completed on schedule by late September 1995 doubling the warehouse and office space.

Lengthy negotiations during 1996 with Capital Cities/ABC to acquire the business and certain assets of the Chilton Book Company, one of the Group's two major US competitors, failed to achieve their objective when the Federal Trade Commission indicated that this would place the Group in a monopoly situation. This abortive acquisition incurred costs of £229,000 which were included in the end of the year results and were offset by making non-recurring economies within the US business.

Sales of used cars were reaching record levels on both sides of the Atlantic, at an estimated six million per year. As the cost of a new car had risen from a quarter of the average US wage packet to almost a third, a used car had become the more attractive option. By the end of the year the increase in turnover of the US companies, now the Group's most profitable subsidiaries, rose by 3 per cent to $12.19 million. Profitability during this period increased by 13 per cent in dollar terms, largely due to the introduction of a third shift in the printing facility, augmented by a move towards longer print runs and the postponement of raw material price increases. The new colour press, mentioned previously, was installed and operational by the end of 1996, to add to the efficiences expected to be realised in the next financial year.

Although trading throughout the year was mixed, the US company profits held up well despite the only modest increase in dollar sales when the last quarter's sales fell below expectations. There was a general decline in consumer spending for three consecutive months caused mainly by poor weather conditions. The Group's pre-tax profits were in line with the original broker's forecast of a 5 per cent increase over the previous year but they were reduced to 2 per cent by the growing strength of the pound. Operating profits of $8.6 million were ahead of 1996 by 16 per cent, encouraged by the doubling of the sales of Spanish language manuals introduced the previous year. The anticipated increase in the cost of offset paper had still failed to materialise but steps were being taken to explore the possibility of using a lighter grade of paper to reduce any future increase to a minimum. Plans for 1998 included placing an order for a second web press to provide further efficiences in line with projected increased volume output.

Autozone, the world's largest automotive parts store chain and the Group's biggest US customer, extended its coverage by acquiring a 112-store chain outlet in New England and followed this up within 12 months with the acquisition of the 560 stores operated by Chief Auto Parts. By the end of 1998 Autozone were well on the way to a store count of 3,000.

The successful launch in November of manuals aimed at the Australasian market produced sales and profits that exceeded their original projections, although a significant fall in the value of the Australian dollar had its effect on the profitability of operations in that country. The important fact was that the Group now had a foothold in the Pacific Rim Region, having commenced trading from a warehouse in Melbourne during November 1997. After allowing for the installation of a new web press in Nashville, the start-up costs of the Australian operation, and an increase in stock levels primarily related to Australia, the US cash situation at the year end was just over $2 million.

As from 22 October 1999, Gordon Stengel assumed the position of Vice President, Sales of Haynes Manuals Inc, taking over from Bill Kilduff who left the company after 15 years, 12 of which he had served as Vice President, Sales. On the same day, Dan Benhardus was promoted to Senior Vice President, Nigel Clements to Vice President Production, and Jim Nicholson to Vice President Finance. During the year, terms were agreed by Haynes Manuals Inc for the acquisition, from a trucking company, of 3.6 acres of property adjacent to the Nashville premises including a 10,000 square foot building. This acquisition will provide future flexibilty for US operations which would otherwise not be available as the existing 4½ acre site had been developed to its maximum.

The Haynes Australian facility outside Melbourne at 34 Jellico Drive, Scoresby, Victoria.

7

The Group goes public

In the same way that the burning ambition of many aspiring motor racing drivers is to compete first of all in club events and then progress to work their way up through Formula Ford to Formula 3, then Formula 2 and eventually to the ultimate form of grand prix circuit racing, Formula 1, it is the ambition of nearly every serious businessman to see his business become listed on the Stock Exchange, or at least to have his shares traded on the AIM or the over-the-counter securities market. Many drivers, such as the late Graham Hill, achieved their objective through sheer determination coupled with the requisite skill, and if the dedicated businessman has the same attributes, he too will realise his goal. To start a company from scratch and to take it public provides the same degree of personal satisfaction that must come from becoming a successful racing driver. Yet as in grand prix racing, the question of timing is critical; if the company is floated too early the benefits may be short-lived, whilst if the move is delayed for too long, it may have passed its peak performance so that it is no longer possible to capitalise fully on its potential.

When going public there is also the question of what route to follow, even after seeking and taking heed of advice offered by those who specialise in such matters. For example, is it prudent to sell out completely for cash or in exchange for equity in the new company, or is it better to be sure of retaining control by disposing of the minimum amount of equity that will satisfy the need for cash, yet still meet the requirements demanded at the time when the company is to be floated on the open market? These and other decisions that needed to be made faced John Haynes when, during 1972 and with the help of his accountant, David Suter, he started to talk to merchant bankers in the City, with the prospect of going public in about three to four years time.

By then he had evolved his own business philosophy from the experience he had gained in running his own company and from observing the activities of others, particularly with regard to how the decisions they made had influenced their subsequent progress. Competitors in particular had their tactics and performance closely monitored, special attention being directed to their profits and turnover, or how any flotations, mergers or acquisitions had affected the company's performance. From this, certain conclusions could be drawn, not the least of which was how easy it was for a businessman to lose control of everything he had built up through an unforeseen change in circumstances that soured a once attractive-looking proposition. To quote John Haynes's words, 'I have yet to meet a man, still involved with his company, who has lost control and remained happy.'

From these and other observations, three salient facts emerged. First, John Haynes had no wish to relinquish control of the companies he had built up, in which he and his family owned 98 per cent of the equity. Secondly, he was convinced that companies that grew organically inevitably ended up in a much stronger position than those that expanded very rapidly by depending upon outside funds. Thirdly, and a view undoubtedly shared by others, he had become aware quite early in his business career that the most vital element in any company is not only the cash at its disposal, or its fixed and current assets, but the people who work in that company. A good, keen, enthusiastic staff will ensure swift progress towards creating a successful enterprise, as he had proved for himself.

Already suffering from the effects of punitive personal taxation, John had reached the point where, although on paper his assets could imply that he was relatively wealthy, in reality there was little cash for him or his family to indulge in some of their fancies and leisure-time pursuits. The continuing growth of the company demanded more working capital, and going public would provide a convenient way in which to raise funds without having to pay high interest rates. Not only would the disposal of equity place a considerable amount of money in the hands of those who released it, but it would also provide a ready market for the company's shares and at the same time place the company in a better position when the need arose to raise further funds for its future development.

Having made the decision to go public, it was important to find a merchant banker that would offer impartial advice and make arrangements for the flotation of shares along the route that had already been decided. Messrs Singer & Friedlander eventually fulfilled this role, making it clear from the very beginning that they would help in whatever way they could, and along whatever route was desired. But before discussions could advance very far, the financial depression of 1974/75 made any question of flotation at that time virtually impossible. Even so, the discussions continued, with regular meetings either in London or at Sparkford. Steady progress was made so that by the end of 1977 it looked as though it would be possible to go public within a couple of years, if this course of action was still desired.

In 1978 the Stock Exchange Council announced that it was lowering its requirement with regard to the minimum amount of equity that needed to be placed on the market when a company was floated. This change provided the necessary incentive to go ahead, with the result that by the middle of that year the Haynes family were in a position to follow the prescribed route for the disposal of a proportion of the equity in the company by selecting one of the three methods that were available to them – a full flotation; the placing of shares without a listing; or the creation and sale of preferred ordinary shares. It was a decision that could be deferred until as late as two weeks prior to the actual sale, since the amount of work that would involve the merchant bank and the investigating accountants and lawyers would be approximately the same, whatever method was selected.

The placing of ordinary shares without a listing seemed the most attractive proposition, as this would permit the sale of as little as 10 per cent of the equity, and provide a sure means of retaining family interests and control. The creation and sale of preferred ordinary shares looked attractive too, but it would have resulted in irksome restrictions being placed on the company's growth if it were to be hit by bad trading patches. It then became apparent that if preferred ordinary shares, or ordinary shares without a listing, were sold, they would need to be discounted to reflect the lack of a proper company listing on the London Stock Exchange. This would not be conducive to getting the best possible price for the minimum requirement after spending something like 20 years building up the company. The advice given showed that only a full flotation following the sale of the minimum 25 per cent of equity would get the right price. Thus it seemed that a full flotation would offer the best advantages, because after the company had been thoroughly vetted by accountants and lawyers, and then exposed to the harsh glare of publicity, the shares sold would achieve a better price than if either of the other routes had been followed.

There were, of course, advantages and disadvantages in selecting any of the options, but the course chosen seemed to offer by far the best compromise. The prestige derived from turning a private company into a public company would more than outweigh any disadvantages caused by exposure in the financial press, and because the company had always been run on conservative lines, there was little danger of a clash of interests between professional fund managers and the entrepreneur running the company. Whilst going public is an expensive way to raise cash for shareholders and create a market in the company's equity, the consideration of getting the best possible price for the shares to be sold would overrule the increase in cost, which in this instance amounted to some £40,000, mostly in newspaper advertising. An interesting advantage in going for a full flotation, with all its attendant publicity, is that the shares are not marketed on the underlying assets of the company, but on the profitability record and the prospect of increases in profitability to follow. Thus the maximum number of potential investors is made aware of what is available and, if there is the offer of sale by tender, they are encouraged to bid what they think the company is worth.

Warning was given that the six months leading up to the flotation would be a very busy period, an understatement at the very least! Although the whole operation was masterminded by Singer & Friedlander Limited under the smooth guidance of their Managing Director, Panton Corbett, it was necessary for the outside auditors to verify the accounts of both the UK and US companies over the past five years, whilst at the same time the company had to make profit projections for its financial year ended 31 May 1980.

Numerous meetings were held, and Singer & Friedlander's advice was accepted in the main, with the result that contact was made not only with first-class professional people, but with people whose company was enjoyed and with whom a very congenial working relationship was developed. Lawyers and brokers were appointed who would handle the share issues and also the Press. L. Messel & Co were selected as brokers, and in the selection of City lawyers D. J. Freeman & Co were chosen. By the end of July 1979 the roles of all the main players had been cast and all the introductions made. It was now the turn of the auditors to spring into action, turning the Accounts Departments in both the UK and the USA completely upside down, for it had been decided that the equity would be sold in the late autumn or possibly in the following spring.

At this stage the UK and US companies were brought together by means of a holding company, so that they were no longer separate entities, this in itself being a major undertaking. Then, from August on, the pace really began to accelerate. The first Prospectus Meeting was held in September, the prospectus being a document that is subject to the most careful scrutiny and

Preparing for the flotation of the new public company in November 1979. Left to right: Neville Sanders, Mr Haynes Snr, Frank Day, John Haynes, David Suter and Annette Haynes.

It is difficult to believe that Mr Haynes Senior, seen in the company of David Suter (left) and John Mead (right), was an octogenarian and still so active. He had the distinction of being Britain's oldest Company Secretary when he was a mere 83!

the most skilful composition. At the end of that meeting a rough draft was available, with various people delegated to fill in the missing areas so that it could be completed and printed. A second meeting followed in October, by which time the draft reports from the accountants had been added in. Progress was sufficiently swift for a meeting to be arranged with John Davies of *The Observer* only a week later, which resulted in a very satisfactory article appearing in the following Sunday's edition. Third and fourth Prospectus Meetings took place during mid-October and early November, the printed proofs being corrected after each, the last meeting culminating in a lunchtime press conference in the offices of the financial advisers. Again, good publicity resulted, one of the newspapers referring to John Haynes's father as the oldest Company Secretary in England – well, he was a sprightly 83!

Even more work was necessary when it came to the production of a document known as Verification Notes, to be presented just three weeks before the offer for sale was due to be made. In this document, every statement or opinion voiced in the Prospectus had to be verified to the satisfaction of the lawyers. The Directors looked with mounting horror through the 84 questions asked over 18 pages of foolscap paper as the complexity of what they were being asked to do became apparent, together with an appreciation of the enormous amount of time and work it was going to take to answer each of the questions properly. These ranged from such questions as 'Please produce any available evidence that sales were made initially by mail order', 'Please produce evidence confirming that the business in North America now accounts for 24 per cent of Group sales', 'Please produce a list of the Group's titles broken down between the five constituent elements', 'Are the Directors satisfied that a manual will enable a user to make virtually any form of repair or maintenance? What maintenance will it *not* enable them to undertake?' to 'Please produce evidence that in 1974 the Group's market share was approximately 35 per cent of the UK market' and so on. Archives were dug into and much midnight oil was burnt, but in the end the answers to all the questions were satisfactorily completed. There followed a visit to the brokers to explain to about 20 members of their company all about the Haynes organisation and its prospects so that they would be well briefed when selling shares to customers. The scene was now set with the underwriting due to take place on 12 November, impact day being on the 14th and completion on the 15th. This meant the offer for sale would have to be published in the newspapers on the 19th.

It was then that a temporary postponement of publication of the offer for sale was suggested by the merchant bankers for a variety of very good reasons, but only for a couple of weeks. Although this created a feeling of great anticlimax, it permitted a fifth and final Prospectus Meeting to be held on 26 November, at which time the minimum offer price of 95p per share was agreed, it having been decided at the initial Prospectus Meeting that the issued share capital would be 5,000,000 ordinary shares of 20p each, and that 1,250,000 of them would be offered for sale by tender. Two days later the Completion Meeting started, finishing on the following day, 29 November. This two-day meeting involved massive signing sessions, the paperwork amounting to a substantially bound volume two inches thick! With the meeting successfully completed, the now totally exhausted participants adjourned to the Savoy Hotel where, at just one minute past midnight, they toasted the Haynes Publishing Group Limited which had just come into existence as a public company. Details of the share offer were published in the press on 3 December, applications for shares to close on the 6th.

Between these two dates were three nerve-wracking days, as it was now the public who were being asked to assess the company and to decide whether their shares were worth at least 95p each, bearing in mind the stated net asset value at that time was 27p per share. This was also an anxious time for the merchant bankers, for they had underwritten the issue, which meant that if some of the shares were not sold, they had guaranteed to buy them at the minimum tender price. The Main Board, comprising John and Annette Haynes, Frank Day, David Suter and John's father, together with Neville Sanders (the Group's long-standing legal advisor), travelled to London on 6 December in a highly apprehensive state. The atmosphere was electric, for at this stage there was no indication of what would be found at the merchant banker's when they arrived there. Would there be glum faces, with the issue being only partly taken up, or would there be smiles and congratulations at the issue having been a success? In the event such was the success of the flotation that the issue had been over-subscribed 13 times, prices ranging from a minimum of 95p to £1.70 per share. To walk into a large room which had been cleared of everything except specially erected trestle tables around the walls was an astounding sight, not to be forgotten. Behind the tables sat some 20 clerks sorting through thousands of applications, each one accompanied by a cheque, placing each application in the correct pile. Over £18,000,000 was banked by Singers that day, prior to returning most of the cash to unsuccessful applicants.

When all the calculations had been made halfway through lunch, it was announced that the minimum price at which all shares would be sold was £1.20 per share, exactly what John had wanted when he started the run up to flotation, yet a figure which, at one time, had been considered highly optimistic! The company's staff were kept fully advised of what was going on and by making application on a special form, had the opportunity of purchasing shares at the minimum offer price of 95p. Over 30 per cent of the employees then owned shares in the company and, it was hoped, had a much better idea of what the business was all about.

A few days later, at the start of the first day of trading, members of the Board had the opportunity to visit the Stock Exchange and go down on the floor to meet the jobbers who had started dealing in the shares, thanks to arrangements made by Messels. To the delight of all, the shares finished the day several pence up.

8

Making headway in difficult times

When the Haynes Publishing Group went public on 29 November 1979 with a full listing on the London Stock Exchange, one of the assumptions included in the prospectus was that sales performance would approximate to that of the previous year. This was not easy to forecast with any confidence because at the time Britain was suffering from its infamous 'stop-go' economy. When the UK inflation rate rose above 20 per cent the forecast started to go awry and was not helped after the US exchange rate had edged down more than 10 per cent by the following May. Other factors were also destined to have their effect on the end-of-year results.

Towards the end of the 1980 financial year an unprecedented and severe reduction of stock held by both retail outlets and wholesalers resulted in substantially reduced orders. The effect was felt mostly in the final quarter of the year when, on previous occasions, there had been a seasonal increase. This unexpected shortfall in sales resulted in profit reduction instead of the usual end-of-the-year uplift. This unexpected setback was compounded by several weeks of industrial action by one of the print unions, the National Graphical Association. It cost the company a loss in production of something like 150,000 books and created an imbalance in stock levels, even though the union had no disagreement with the company.

In the USA the setting up of an editorial team at Newbury Park had taken place on a much larger scale than originally envisaged, creating a correspondingly larger rise in origination costs. The decision to take this action despite the current poor state of the UK market could be more than justified in view of the considerable potential for the expansion of business in the USA. As subsequent events were to show, it had been the correct action to take.

When making an analysis of the year-end results it had to be borne in mind that the company had adopted an unusual and conservative method of accounting by writing-off against profit all the origination costs of new titles in the year in which they had been incurred, often before any sales of the titles concerned had been realised. This resulted in a high break even point, but meant that after this point had been reached, some 60 per cent of sales revenue flowed straight through to profit, the manufacturing costs being comparatively low. Taking the 1980 financial year as an example, the additional cost of origination amounted to approximately £182,000, a total of £493,000 being spent that year, compared with £311,000 in 1979, all of which had been written off on the profit and loss account.

Despite the continuing recession in the UK and the resultant economic gloom that had set the scene, the company's 1981 annual report inspired confidence and augured well for their 21st Anniversary year. Sales had increased by 16.6 per cent and the profit before taxation was up by 16.3 per cent. Most of this year's growth had been generated within the home market due to the combined effects of the end of retail and wholesale destocking, the publication of new titles and the acquisition of new accounts.

The 1982 annual report showed that Group turnover had increased by 15.3 per cent when compared with the previous year's figure and that profit before taxation had increased by 18.9 per cent. Growth was now evident in the USA as well as in the UK, the former company having nearly doubled its profitability when compared with the 1981 figure. Although fierce competition continued in the US market, America was now also emerging from the recessionary period that had seriously affected its motor manufacturers, amongst others.

Steady progress was confirmed when the 1983 Annual Report was published. Turnover had increased by 15.4 per cent and pre-tax profitability was up by 25.6 per cent. In percentage terms G. T. Foulis had shown the greatest rate of growth due to increasing penetration of the traditional book trade. This included sales to book clubs and confirmed the editorial selection and planning of new titles had been good.

A major step towards consolidating the Group's activities on the Sparkford site had been achieved when the 14,500 square foot warehouse mentioned in the 1983 annual report had been completed in October that year. It had the capacity to stock up to 1.2 million books for distribution to the south of England and the very latest in stock selection equipment. A further 3,000 square feet of office accommodation was also being built so that the Sales and Marketing Department could return from temporary exile in Ilchester. As soon as the new warehouse was operational, the book stock in Yeovil was transferred there and the 9,000 square foot Goldcroft warehouse vacated. The book stock had been relocated there when the premises in Park Road had earlier been closed and the Accounts Department had moved back to Sparkford. By running three lorries non-stop between Sparkford and Yeovil the complete stock of 400,000 books was transferred during a weekend in November. When the Haynes Publishing Group signs had been taken down from the two now-vacant premises in Yeovil, a rumour quickly spread around the area that the company was in decline. There are always 'dismal Jimmies' around and one of them went so far as to say 'I knew it would never last!'. Fortunately, when the end-of-the-year results were published in the local newspaper, they told a completely different story.

Additional staff taken on by the Production Department led to a notable achievement in the 1983/84 financial year when over 100,000 books were produced and bound in one week. This was reflected in an increase in profits before taxation of 22 per cent, with turnover up by 15 per cent. (Today, the average production is more than 150,000 books per week in total from both Sparkford and Nashville.) For the first time the Group had spent just over £1 million during the year on origination. To sustain the company's growth through its own efforts an even busier new book programme was envisaged for the following year, with an increase in senior staffing levels to deal with the additional workload.

The Oxford Illustrated Press imprint now showed in percentage terms the greatest increase in sales and profitability. G. T. Foulis also enjoyed a most successful year. New and updated *Owners Workshop Manuals* for cars and motorcycles, and handbooks for the former, from both the UK and the USA, continued to make by far the largest contribution to the Group's profitability. They were the core of the Group's business and would remain the main contributor to its continuing success.

The formation of Camway Autographics Limited during January 1984 provided the opportunity to handle advertising for not only the Group but also for third parties. Within a year of occupying the then unused office space at Ivel House, Ilchester, they were able to move into 3,000 square feet of

A scene of complete devastation. Site preparation prior to the erection of the new Southern Area Distribution Depot at Sparkford, in the area that once contained the old Dutch barn.

The new warehouse begins to take shape at Sparkford with the erection of the structural steelwork. Height is an important factor in this case to permit high racking to be used in conjunction with a specially designed fork lift truck.

purpose-built office accommodation at the Haynes Motor Museum, close to the main Sparkford site. Here they had the added advantages of access to a boardroom and a conference centre.

An interesting development that came to fruition during 1984 was the production for the first time of 'own branded' workshop manuals for a major multinational car manufacturer in the UK. At more or less the same time the Dutch language rights were licensed to Kluwer, one of the biggest publishers in the Netherlands, the books being printed in the Dutch language at Sparkford. For some time translation rights for manuals had been licensed to overseas publishers but to have the opportunity also of printing the foreign language edition represented the beginning of another significant breakthrough.

Successful negotiations with Penguin Books during 1985 led to the

The completed warehouse. Ron Tucker sees one of the company's trucks on its way with yet another consignment of books.

When the Park Road premises were finally vacated and the signs removed, local rumour suggested that the Haynes Publishing Group was facing hard times. The company's Annual Report told quite a different story!

purchase of all 64 titles of Frederick Warne's transport list, subsequently to be marketed and republished under the G. T. Foulis imprint. Penguin wished to retain the Warne name for all the other titles that remained with them on that imprint's back list.

In the UK motor accessory trade losses due to unforeseen bankruptcies increased during the 1984/85 financial year and sent a shock wave throughout the automotive aftermarket. The liquidation of one chain of motor accessory

Haynes Publishing sponsored the Sparkford Cricket Club's match against the Somerset County team in 1983, when James Hunt was the guest of honour. He is seen here with John Haynes and Murray Corfield.

shops alone created a deficit of over £20 million to its many suppliers. It was fortunate that at the time of the crash prudent action by the Accounts and Sales departments had reduced the company's risk to only a minimal involvement. Profits before taxation were up by an encouraging 24 per cent, whilst turnover showed an 18 per cent increase over that of the previous year.

To meet increasing demand from home and abroad for the next three years, the production and printing area in the Sparkford factory was being increased by a further 4,500 square feet and nearing completion. The five-colour computer-controlled press purchased during early 1984 was now installed and producing work of excellent quality that enabled general throughput to increase. New laser-based photo-typesetting equipment had also been installed and brought on line. Already it was showing benefits in both speed and economy.

Breach of copyright overseas is often difficult to track down and even more difficult to prove as the law is rather vague in some areas. When a Finnish publisher was found to have reproduced Haynes illustrative material without permission and refused to acknowledge the claim for recompense, legal proceedings were instituted. The court case that followed upheld the claim and the three presiding Finnish judges imposed a heavy fine on the Finnish publishers.

Another new subsidiary company came into being during 1985 – Haynes Garages Limited – to facilitate the purchase of vehicles for research and also for the Group's own fleet. The company by now had its own trade

The Haynes Publishing Group PLC Main Board in April 1985. Left to right: Jim Scott, David Suter (in attendance), Annette Haynes, John Haynes, David Haynes and Max Pearce. The other Non-Executive Director, David Quayle, was absent on this occasion. Taking the minutes is Liz Trim.

plates so that cars and motorcycles could be road tested at the conclusion of the stripdown and rebuild that formed the basis of every new workshop manual. Many of the cars were subsequently used by the company's senior management and it is a tribute to the skill of the workshop mechanics that they subsequently gave long and reliable service.

Employees stood to gain a further benefit that year by the introduction of a profit-sharing scheme. With the first payment to be made in November 1985, the objective was to provide additional incentives based on increases in the overall profitability and the performance of the companies. The US companies, which had their own employee benefit plan, were not eligible for inclusion in the UK scheme.

Also in 1985, the Group celebrated its 25th Anniversary and by coincidence, it was also the centenary year of the motor car. The occasion was marked by a display of the Group's products at Silverstone race circuit where the Motor 100 celebrations were staged 25–27 May.

The 4,500 square foot extension to the Sparkford factory had been completed on schedule during the year and the web presses relocated, so there was now space for a new bindery machine. The installation of the Kolbus bindery line, the first of its kind in the world, would enable production to be doubled up to the year 1992, and possibly beyond. The old bindery was retained in a back-up role. Extra office accommodation had been created by a new 3,000 square foot mezzanine floor at one end of the Southern Area Distribution Depot. It was used to accommodate the Sales

The J. H. Haynes & Co Ltd Board in April 1985. Left to right: Andy Lynch, Pete Ward, Annette Haynes, Liz Trim taking the minutes, Jim Scott, David Haynes, Roger Stagg, Peter Bishop and Jeff Clew. John Haynes was absent on this occasion.

and Marketing Department and the G. T. Foulis Editorial Department.

Publication of the 1986 Annual Report revealed a further increase in turnover, which was offset by an overall decrease in profits on trading of 8.4 per cent. This was despite sales from the UK-based operating company being well ahead of expectations and the acquisition of further major accounts. Amongst other factors the strengthening of the pound in relation to the dollar by about 18 per cent had nullified the 13.9 per cent gain in sales enjoyed by the US company. Furthermore, the continuing decline in the UK motorcycle market still gave rise for concern, with sales of motorcycle manuals reflecting this downward trend. The decline in new motorcycle sales seemed likely to continue in the foreseeable future, making the G. T. Foulis and Oxford Illustrated Press imprints the second-most important sector of the business.

On 23 August 1985 Max Pearce was appointed Executive Vice Chairman of Haynes Publications Inc and became an Executive Director on the Group's Main Board. Max Pearce had had a 20-year career with Halfords, rising from Management Trainee to a Main Board Director. He was the third generation of his family to work for Halfords. Max was the founder of Maccess, the market leading automotive cash and carry wholesale group. At the time of his appointment, Halfords and Maccess were the first and second largest customers of the Haynes Group worldwide. In the 1980s, Max had moved to GKN Auto Parts International where, as Deputy Managing Director, he was involved in the development of parts distribution around the world – USA, Australia, France and the UK. From 1988 until 1992 he was a director of Granada Leisure and Managing Director of Lakewoods, a joint venture company between Granada and John Laing to develop high quality holiday villages in the UK.

A month earlier, in July 1985, Pete O'Donohue had been appointed as President of Haynes Publications Inc. Jim Scott, by now the Managing Director of J. H. Haynes & Co Ltd, was appointed to the Main Board during the summer.

In December 1985, Jeff Clew, the Group's Executive Editorial Director, was presented with the 1985 Guild of Motoring Writers' Montagu Trophy. It is awarded annually to the Guild member 'who, in the opinion of the nominated jury, has made the greatest contribution to recording in the English language the history of motoring or motorcycling in a published book or article, a film, television or radio script, or in a research manuscript available to the public.' It was the first time it had been awarded for a motorcycle-related subject, this being his book *JAP: The Vintage Years*, published by G. T. Foulis.

An uncharacteristically poor performance during the first half of the 1986/87 financial year was countermanded by an anticipated recovery in the second half, mainly US-inspired following the appointment of Englishman Eric Oakley as the President of the US company. Record profits were achieved, up 21 per cent on an increased turnover of 13 per cent on the previous year.

The Guild of Motoring Writers' Montagu Trophy, presented to Jeff Clew in December 1985 in recognition of his book, *JAP: The Vintage Years* (published under the G. T. Foulis imprint) as the 'greatest contribution to motoring and motorcycle history' that year. Several other Haynes authors appear in the list of previous winners.

In May 1987 the Oxford Publishing Company (OPC) imprint was acquired, a company that specialised in railway subjects. The entire stock and rights in the 200 or so different titles published by this company were purchased by a cash transaction from Cassell PLC. Wherever possible the production of reprints and new titles under the OPC imprint, from typesetting to binding, would be carried out by Group companies to effect further economies. Peter Nicholson had earlier been appointed Editor at Haynes to create the company's own list of railway titles, so this acquisition was particularly well-timed.

During the year David Quayle, a Non-Executive Director, resigned from the Main Board on 31 May to take up the Chairmanship of Granada Leisure. A new web press costing £237,000 was acquired and installed during the autumn to increase production capacity and maintain the high print quality of the Group's books.

For the 1987/88 financial year record profits showed an increase of 36 per cent over those achieved the previous year. This increase was achieved on a turnover that was up by 14 per cent. UK turnover increased by 15 per cent. Whilst the core of the business remained in the publication of car and motorcycle workshop manuals, the three other imprints – G. T. Foulis, the Oxford Illustrated Press, and the specialist railway imprint Oxford Publishing Company, all made a particularly significant contribution. A new annual publication, the *Automotive Technical Data Book*, made its debut during the year, a reference work aimed specifically at the garage trade. There was only one other such publication on the market at the time, which sold in

Oxford Publishing Company (OPC) has always been a highly regarded specialist railway imprint and during its time as part of the Haynes Publishing Group some interesting book launches were organised. This particular occasion was tinged with sadness however as the author, Robert Adley MP, had died suddenly just before his book, *Countdown to 1968*, was published in 1993. Members of the Haynes staff pose with invited journalists and, third from left, Mrs Jane Adley and centre, Haynes Director, David Suter. The locomotive is GWR 'Modified Hall' class 4-6-0 No 6998 *Burton Agnes Hall* and is at Bury Bolton Street station on the East Lancashire Railway.
(Peter Nicholson)

Haynes Manuals on a conveyor belt in the Bindery Department, Sparkford, October 1987.

An aerial view of the Sparkford site, October 1987.

sufficiently large numbers to make a rival publication attractive. To get the first issue of such a comprehensive publication under way proved very labour-intensive and continued to be so until its content could be computerised. The project was masterminded by Julian McGeoch and its immediate success encouraged the Group to look at other projected titles for this segment of the marketplace.

Work had commenced on a new 14,000 square foot two-storey building on the Sparkford site to extend production facilities still further. The web press mentioned previously was now up and running and another had been installed early in the new year. A further 10,000 square foot press hall would soon be under construction to link the new building with the main factory.

In the USA, a new 36,000 square foot warehouse in Nashville, Tennessee had been purchased at the end of the financial year. Occupying a freehold site of 4.5 acres, it was completed on schedule and within budget to become fully operational on 13 June 1988. An investment of this magnitude by a British company was welcomed by the Governor of the State of Tennessee, Ned McWherter, who officially opened the new warehouse during November 1988. Earlier he had visited the Group's headquarters at Sparkford and during his visit unveiled a plaque on their new two-storey building.

Because of an increasingly busy publishing programme in which 171 new titles had been produced, record consolidated pre-tax profits were up by 10 per cent on those of the previous year, as confirmed in the 1989 Annual Report. Turnover had increased by 16 per cent. As the Group had made unprecedented levels of investment both in the UK and the USA it was decided to revert to the publishing industry's customary policy on writing off origination costs. They would no longer be written off during the year in which they were incurred but, instead, over the life of the first print run or five years, whichever came first. To provide comparable figures, the 1988 figures were restated as if this policy had also applied until then. Car and motorcycle *Owners Workshop Manuals* were now being distributed through the book trade as well as the automobile market to increase the number of outlets in the UK. Further garage trade publications had been developed this year such as the *Tyre Pressure and Wheel Manual* and books on topics such as fuel injection and diesel engines. G. T. Foulis, the Oxford Illustrated Press and the Oxford Publishing Company continued to make an increased contribution to the Group's strength in the 1988/89 financial year. Not to be overlooked was the way in which business was developing in the UK export market. It applied to all countries outside North America, sales in Europe, Scandanavia, Australia and New Zealand having been particularly encouraging.

The new two-storey building at Sparkford was now complete and work had begun on the 10,000 square foot press hall to link it to the main factory. This was to house the second new five-colour Heidelberg SRA1 computer-controlled offset litho press already on order and due to be installed during January 1990 at a cost of £750,000. The new press would take a sheet size

The framework of the 14,000 square foot two-storey building at Sparkford, November 1988.

twice that of the existing colour press, and more than double the Group's colour printing capacity. These new facilities would provide the extra capacity for all new titles to be produced in-house.

Camway Autographics Limited had taken a major step forward in the spring of 1989 with the acquisition and installation of a comprehensive computer-aided graphic design system. It enabled them to improve overall efficiency and to expand their client base.

Continuing capital expenditure on new buildings, plant and equipment had been at heavy cash cost to the UK business which had taken short-term loans from the banks to supplement the normally positive cash flow. With the programme scheduled for completion by the spring of 1990 it would put the company in an excellent position to expand still further as a publisher and producer of high-quality books.

The acquisition of Regency Reprographics (Bath) Limited during the 1989/90 financial year provided the ability to produce books with more colour pages. Regency Reprographics was in a loss-making situation at the time of purchase but it was expected this could be turned round to make a useful contribution to the Group by the end of the year.

After the year's end three separate parcels of land and buildings adjoining the company's main headquarters at Sparkford were purchased when they came up for sale unexpectedly. It provided the opportunity to concentrate all the UK company's production activities on the Sparkford site. A bookshop in Oxford was purchased and renamed CATBAP (Cars and Trains, Boats and Planes) and was run by Jonathan Tomlinson, a very experienced transport bookshop manager. It got off to a good start by exceeding its budget within a couple of months of opening. The upstairs rooms also provided accommodation for the Oxford Illustrated Press editorial office.

Included in the purchase of property and land at Sparkford was Golden Quoins, a bungalow which had to be extensively modified before Camway Autographics could be accommodated. Unfortunately, the floor space of the bungalow was approximately half of what was needed and when this was made evident they were asked to come up with a plan for extending the building. Thereby hangs a tale. The plan needed to be drawn up at very short notice in time for it to be discussed at the next Main Board meeting. As a result it took the form of an 'over the top' design for a futuristic building, intended mainly to stimulate discussion. Camway had been led to believe that action would be deferred for three months but when enquiries were made, they were told their concept had been approved two days previously and work would commence the following week! Some six to nine months later the two-storey building had been completed and they were able to move in on 8 October 1990.

The capital expenditure programme, together with stock increases in

A copyproof camera in operation, Sparkford, April 1989.

The remarkable transformation of a domestic bungalow into a modern office and studio building – during and after. Previously known as Golden Quoins, this is now the Sparkford home of the Design Department.

the USA, had by now boosted borrowings to such a high level that the Group did not expect to discharge its debts completely for several years, but a fifth consecutive year of uninterrupted growth was the highlight of the 1989/90 financial year.

As difficult trading conditions continued in the UK, the strategy had been to limit exposure in the home market by further growth in the USA. Conditions for traders in the UK remained difficult, and the percentage increase in turnover was low, due to the effects the high interest rates and revisions of the uniform business rate had on customers. The failure of another one of the company's biggest automotive customers, Spice PLC, gave rise to some disruption throughout the automotive aftermarket, although eventually the business lost was gradually absorbed by the remainder of the trade.

On 10 May 1990 David Suter, who was in practice as a chartered accountant on his own account and a former partner in Baker Tilley, was appointed a Non-Executive Director on the Main Board. On 22 June Eric Oakley, the President of Haynes Publications Inc, was also appointed a Director on the Group's Main Board.

At the annual general meeting held on 25 October 1990 a resolution was passed which gave shareholders the option of receiving their dividends wholly or partly in New Ordinary Shares rather than in cash. This was because it had become obvious that the temporary reversal in the Group's normally positive cash flow would continue for perhaps another year. This followed an earlier resolution passed at an extraordinary general meeting held on 26 October the previous year. It had authorised the company to increase their share capital by the creation of 6 million new 20p shares in the expectation that the increase in the number of ordinary shares and the consequent reduction in the market price per share would lead to the improved marketability of ordinary shares for shareholders. It doubled the number of shares in issue and paved the way for the directors to offer the choice of receiving cash or ordinary shares for all or part of the final dividend and any dividend declared before the next annual general meeting.

The first line of the Chairman's statement in the 1990/91 interim report was that Group turnover had increased by almost 20 per cent during the first six months of the financial year. Immediately below it came the bad news. A recession had struck both the UK and the US markets, seriously reducing the Group's profitability. It had decreased by 70.2 per cent compared with the same period in the previous year. The recession had dealt the Group a devastating blow at a time when it was at its most vulnerable.

9

Recession – and recovery

The 1990 financial year had started off with promise, the expansion of the factory and the production element of the UK company having been completed in good time. Furthermore, another imprint had been acquired, Patrick Stephens Limited, which had been purchased from HarperCollins for £750,000. With the acquisition came Darryl Reach, a co-founder of the company with Patrick Stephens in 1967, who brought with him considerable publishing expertise. Initially the company was located in the offices on the Haynes Motor Museum site, about a quarter of a mile from the Group headquarters in Sparkford.

When the recession struck, it hit the Haynes Publishing Group with devastating suddenness, like so many other businesses, and caught them unawares. Elsewhere, banks called in loans so that many businesses went bankrupt almost overnight or struggled desperately in a depressed marketplace just to survive. Throughout Britain, home owners found themselves in a perilous position too. Many of those made redundant had difficulty in repaying their mortgages and with plummeting house prices were either forced into negative equity or had their homes repossessed as the banks and building societies foreclosed. Personnel managers were deluged with job applications when any vacancy was advertised and when older people were laid off they found they had become unemployable overnight.

The recession's immediate impact on the Group became apparent to the outside world when the results for the year ending 31 May 1991 were announced. Jim Scott earlier in the year had reported to the other directors that the sales achieved in the middle of 1990 represented the lowest monthly figures recorded since June 1984 and was asked what remedial action he proposed to take. Obviously one of the major priorities in the UK would be to slow down the production of books, which would not only reduce the cost of holding finished stock but also that of raw materials. Yet as Jim pointed out, even a publishing programme reduced to nine new titles a month from January 1991 would still lead to more being produced in 1990/91 than in 1989/90. Max Pearce was of the opinion that the editorial situation as a whole should be reviewed, with contracted but not yet published titles all being subjected to revised viability assessments being prepared by Keith Fullman. A careful re-assessment had shown that, while the workshop manuals remained highly profitable, the book trade imprints had been losing money for some time. An immediate problem was the huge overstock of these books, necessitating some serious remaindering.

David Haynes had already stated he believed the starting place for any cohesive plan would be to reduce the UK company's fixed cash costs, from which the minimum level of sales and production activity could then be determined. From such a beginning the directors could then formulate a plan to head off a projected deficit of £6 million, bearing in mind the Group had previously negotiated facilities for a total borrowing of only £5 million. Discussions about divisionalising the company had been initiated by David Haynes during the late 1980s, his objective being to demonstrate the true performance of individual parts of the business, and particularly whether it would be more profitable to buy in finished book trade books instead of making them in-house. Much of the subsequent preparatory work had been carried out by Alan Sperring, to be taken up by Keith Fullman, a chartered accountant with experience in developing businesses, when he joined the company during August 1990 as Group Strategic Planner. Divisionalisation was later also touched upon at a series of strategic development meetings organised by Max Pearce when key members of the UK company were freely able to express their own opinions for the first time.

The Main Board agreed that in the first instance a complete hold should be put on the publication programme for February and March 1991, a reduction should be made in the workforce, and it was needed to establish what plant and equipment could be sold. Any capital expenditure including the replacement of company vehicles would have to be postponed for the immediate future. At the current exchange rate profit was being lost by producing manuals in the UK for the US market. Max Pearce advised that Eric Oakley had found a printer in California who could provide a considerable saving to the US business in printing manuals if this work were to be undertaken in the USA. He had been asked to obtain a detailed estimate of costs for a wide variety of print runs and pages, which subsequently showed that a reduction in costs could be achieved. Arrangements were made for an initial run by Griffin Printing of Los Angeles to evaluate its quality. Moving some printing away from Sparkford would of course increase the cost of production in the UK, but the net result for the Group as a whole would be beneficial.

It was agreed that to conserve cash, new shares should be offered instead of cash for the 1990 final dividend and so many shareholders accepted the offer that application was made to the London Stock Exchange for 99,743 new ordinary shares to be listed. The figures for book trade sales and those of the workshop manuals in the UK were seen to be very disappointing and down on forecast by almost 13 per cent. Just over 55,000 G. T. Foulis and almost 12,000 Oxford Illustrated Press books had been remaindered to bring in cash. Although in recent years the output of US-originated motorcycle manuals had ceased in order to give the automobile manuals precedence, it was agreed the situation in the USA should be reviewed since America was also suffering from a depressed market situation similar to that in the UK. The outcome was that two ex-Clymer authors were commissioned to bring the range of US titles up to date and to originate new titles on the larger-capacity imported models that were now dominating the US motorcycle market.

David Haynes recommended to the other directors that no interim dividend payment be made to save in the region of £425,000 in cash but in the end an interim dividend of 1p per share was made for the six-month period ended 30 November 1990. The year-long search to replace Shearson Lehman Hutton as the Group's stockbrokers resulted in the appointment of Beeson Gregory, who specialised in smaller public companies. This action was agreed at the following board meeting, to take effect from 31 December 1990.

Max Pearce was of the opinion that the Group's long-term objective should be to add additional warehousing space at Sparkford so that the Leeds warehouse could be closed and the Vehicle Research Workshop transferred from Wincanton to the Sparkford site. This action would ensure that all aspects of the UK operation were concentrated in the one area. The Research Workshop had been moved to a Wincanton trading estate during an earlier expansion at Sparkford and it was in this workshop that cars and motorcycles were stripped and rebuilt for workshop manual projects.

When all the stock from the Leeds warehouse was transferred to the Southern Area Distribution Depot at Sparkford the latter would need to have its staffing complement increased. This could be achieved by diverting the

The UK company has run a suggestions scheme for many years, now known as 'Innovations', in which staff are encouraged to put forward ideas for improving efficiency and cost savings. This is the occasion of the first cash award made after the launch of the scheme, this being for a suggestion in connection with marketing workshop manuals. Left to right: Terry Mitchell, Personnel Manager, Jim Scott, Managing Director, Peter Nicholson, Editor and Rod Grainger, Editorial Director, Book Trade Division.

excess bindery staff to fulfil this function, who otherwise would have faced redundancy. The Board agreed that Ron Encell, the Manager of the Leeds warehouse, should be given the opportunity of closing it as soon as possible and overseeing the transfer of its content to Sparkford. Murray Corfield, a director of Haynes Developments Limited, a privately owned family property company, was instructed to search for suitable leasehold storage space within the immediate vicinity of Sparkford as the stock from Leeds would completely overwhelm the amount of vacant storage space currently available on the Sparkford site. Before the Leeds warehouse closed the Board would decide how best to deal with the 'dead' and slow-moving stock held there, to see whether it was worth the expenditure in bringing it back to Somerset.

By the time of the December 1990 board meeting, some 24,000 square feet of warehousing accommodation available to rent had been found in Wincanton, with three years of the previous tenant's lease still to run. David Suter noted the stock appeared to have increased by £1 million during the year and to meet this problem it was agreed that slow-selling workshop manual titles should be cut from the list temporarily and that the length of print runs should be reduced. It was also agreed that the printing of book trade books should stop if the paper had not yet been purchased and that only the titles that were expected to sell exceptionally well should be produced.

The situation had worsened by the time of the February board meeting, when Jim Scott reported that the sales volumes of workshop manuals had missed the revised forecast by almost 3 per cent and were about 15 per cent behind the total achieved in the same month the previous year. His main area of concern remained the sales volumes of the book trade imprints. All had shown shortfalls on their individual forecasts both on a monthly and a year-to-date basis. The Board acknowledged that the full effects of the recession in the UK were now being reflected in the downturn of sales in retail outlets.

Action had now to be taken swiftly to reduce operating costs in the UK by cutting the publication programme drastically for all imprints, with the exception of the workshop manuals. This would necessitate the immediate loss of between 10 and 15 members of the workforce in the production area. Any delay would result in the cost of these redundancies having to be carried forward into the 1991/92 financial year. It would also be necessary to cut the general book trade publishing programme for 1991/92 by a half, giving rise to a number of editorial staff redundancies. The Chairman found these to be particularly painful and upsetting as on so many occasions he had paid tribute to the very loyal and hard-working employees to whom the Group owed so much of its success. However, he realised that the survival of the company had to be given priority and that such drastic action was the only way.

In reducing the general book trade publishing programme by half, well in excess of 100 titles were affected. All were under contract, some with work in progress; it cost little short of £500,000 to abort these titles in a fair and professional manner.

The Leeds warehouse closed at the end of January 1991 and all its staff were made redundant. Effective from 4 February all orders were fulfilled from Sparkford. The closure of the Leeds warehouse, with the accompanying reduction in wages and operating costs, saved £200,000, which swelled the total saving to £350,000 a year. As it was no longer necessary to maintain and run a fleet of vehicles after the closure this would represent a further saving. The trucks were sold off and parcel carriage contracted to Securicor. More small orders could now be despatched by Securicor as a result of the changing nature of that company's business which would result in a further annual saving of £150,000.

The Chairman and his wife gave the Board a brief overview of the results of their recent visit to Australia and New Zealand, where they had various meetings with customers and updated themselves on the potential market for the Group's products. Gregory Scientific Manuals had been found to be the market leader in Australia due to their coverage of indigenous vehicles and the large number of titles on their list. The Chairman believed a small warehouse in a major population area would help to achieve greater sales for the Group's products as well as being a useful source of advice about the addition of new titles. It would also avoid delays in supply from the UK which, because of the lengthy sea journey, could take many weeks.

On a year-to-year basis, sales volumes of Patrick Stephens titles had fallen nearly 42 per cent behind their forecast and it was agreed that efforts should be concentrated on improving the imprint's performance. In this respect Darryl Reach had found himself in an unenviable position as the company had been acquired by the Group only to be hit by the full weight of the recession a month later! Quite apart from having to bring all the company's production outwork in-house he had also to cut its publication programme. To then have all this work carried out by the Group proved more costly at that time and this had added to the problems.

At a previous board meeting, when the December figures had been reviewed, it was agreed that the Chairman would speak to Panton Corbett, Managing Director of merchant bankers Singer & Friedlander specifically about the poor figures submitted to support the bank's loan. There was need to explain that two of the ratios they had requested could not be met due to the poor sales performance of the operating company. At the March 1991 meeting, David Haynes expressed concern that because Singer & Friedlander's parameters had been contravened they might exercise their right to convert their loan into a shareholding, fears that fortunately were not realised. Instead, Singer & Friedlander were insisting that the technical default on the £3 million loan be corrected. As the Board continued to be in default on three of the criteria, this placed the company in a much weaker position as the loan facility could be withdrawn and the company put into receivership. The Board agreed that the only option now was to reduce stock levels further by remaindering titles at profit.

Jim Scott brought the company up to date on the remainder situation.

Between 60,000 and 70,000 books were going out early the following week to produce a revenue to be recorded in the April figures. It subsequently amounted to £82,000 which represented a profit of £65,700 and reduced the year-to-date loss to £124,400.

With regard to redundancies, non-union employees had left the company within a few days of the announcement being made. The number from the beginning of the year would total approximately 55 and the saving to the Group on the year-to-year basis would be approximately £600,000.

At a board meeting held at the end of May 1991, it was announced that Singer & Friedlander had asked for a mortgage debenture on all the company's properties which were freehold and owned by the Group. At the following board meeting held during June, it was recorded that the UK company had lost £266,000 in the 1990/91 financial year as opposed to a budgeted profit figure of £3,015,000. Car manufacturers had reported unit sales 25 per cent below those of 1990 due to the recession and there had been a corresponding reduction in the volume of second-hand car sales. This inevitably reflected in a decrease in sales of the Group's main product line, the *Owners Workshop Manuals*. As planned borrowings had increased faster than anticipated, the high rate of interest in the UK alone had accounted for an additional cost of £350,000.

When the figures for the year were finally announced at the beginning of September 1991, the first paragraph in the Chairman's statement read: 'The Group effectively broke even in the year to 31 May 1991 by recording a profit before taxation of £26,000 compared with £3,098,000 the previous year. Group turnover, however, increased by 16 per cent in the full year to £19.2 million due to sales growth in North America and the acquisition of Patrick Stephens in the UK.' He also admitted that with the benefit of hindsight the Board had been slow to respond to the intensity and speed of the UK recession. The reduction of UK costs in response to the recession and the curtailment of the further expansion into general publishing should have begun much earlier.

Action could now be taken to implement the divisionalisation plan, to create the Motor Trade Division, the Special Interest Publishing Division and the Production Division. Although not strictly a division, a similar accounting procedure would be adopted to record general overheads. All would perform a self-accounting function. It was fortuitous that the divisionalisation plan model had been formulated at an earlier date and that, by coincidence, it was ready for adoption at the time when it was most needed. It subsequently confirmed the workshop manuals were still the Group's core product and unlikely to be rivalled in profit terms by the general books.

Confidence in the Group's future was restored in the City by the appointment of Max Pearce as Group Chief Executive in the knowledge that he had been responsible for the real reorganisation of the US company's activities, now the most profitable part of the Group. By implementing a cost reduction and restructuring plan he now aimed to restore the rest of the

Group to higher levels of profitability. A further appointment followed in October when Keith Fullman was appointed to the Main Board as Group Financial Director.

Good progress had been made in the USA, with a continual increase in market share, despite difficult trading conditions. To serve the burgeoning North American market more effectively a new company, Haynes North America Inc, was formed. It would have responsibility for the US publishing programme, Haynes Publications Inc retaining the distribution business.

The 1992 financial year showed a substantial improvement in Group pre-tax profits and consolidated Group borrowings, largely due to the efforts of the Group's American subsidiary. By far the greatest achievement was the UK reduction in net borrowings, which had fallen from £3.8 million in May 1991 to £1.6 million in May 1992. They now represented only 14 per cent of capital, as compared with the 1991 figure of 47 per cent. Most of this being attributable to reducing costs and stock, and by a reduction in capital expenditure.

Regrettably, these measures had also necessitated the need to make a quarter of the UK workforce redundant, which had its effect in all areas of the business – administration, editorial and production. Although the cost of taking this action amounted to £528,000, it was more than counterbalanced by a £1 million per annum saving in wage costs. As a further move towards cost reduction it was decided, where practicable, to put production of all the general publishing work out to tender. To take up the unused in-house capacity a contract printing operation, headed by Pete Vallis, was set up to take on outside work. Ironically, the quality of the company's colour work had been officially marked during the year when it was awarded membership of the Fine Art Trade Guild in recognition of work produced to the high standards expected by the art world.

Inevitably, changes had been made in what was now the Production Division, mostly in the pre-press section. The original typesetting, layout and graphics departments were merged into a single, multi-skilled facility. With modern technology and traditional skills sitting alongside each other, the company now benefited from a hitherto unknown degree of flexibility.

Typesetting and page make-up was now accomplished electronically by a sophisticated AppleMac computer system which had replaced the older, outdated CAPS equipment. All film output work was to be handled by the Odcombe Press, a subsidiary of the US company formed in Nashville to undertake US printing. It ensured that the maximum use was made of their imagesetter to effect further economies and at the same time help to offset its $165,000 cost. Platemaking, however, was to continue at Sparkford, as before.

With the UK economy still in recession, trading conditions remained difficult. Uncertainty surrounding the forthcoming general election in the second half of the year contributed to a 14 per cent fall in turnover compared with the first six months. As a result, turnover for the UK companies rose by only 5 per cent during the year, excluding sales made to the USA.

Interestingly, the reorganisation plan announced the previous year achieved an increase in profit before exceptional items of 314 per cent.

In August 1991, Darryl Reach was appointed Editorial Director of the Special Interest Publishing Division, with responsibility for all book trade imprints. Rod Grainger had left to start his own book publishing venture, and the departure of Jane Marshall led to the winding down of the Oxford Illustrated Press as a move toward imprint rationalisation. Following the reorganisation of the Editorial Departments in 1991, Penny Cox was promoted to Motorcycle Editorial Manager, a post she holds to this day, which gives her complete responsibility for the origination of motorcycle manuals in the UK. Penny had joined Haynes in May 1979 as a young editorial assistant and rose through the ranks to become an Editor in 1987, working under the guidance of Jeff Clew.

Graham Cook joined the company during February 1992 as Marketing Executive–France, to oversee an attempt to penetrate the French car workshop manual market. As a French linguist with previous experience of the French motor industry aftermarket his appointment coincided with the imminent launch of 12 French language titles. The launch took place a couple of months later, aimed at building up new markets for the Group. The workshop manual is a repeatable formula and translating it into foreign languages helps to maximise the return on the original investment and to provide the Group with a stronger international base. Contrary to the previous practice of selling the translation rights, the French language manuals had been translated and printed in-house. They were distributed to the hypermarkets and French motor accessory shops by Mecanoto of Lyon.

The final stage in the transfer of the UK company's 'outposts' took

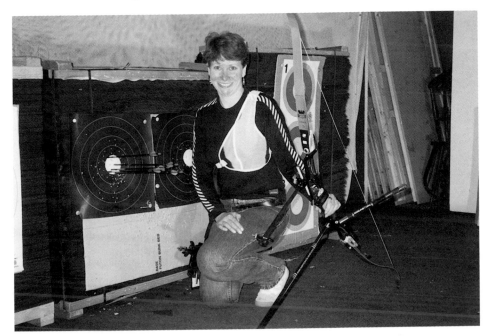

Motorcycle Editorial Manager Penny Cox, who has been with the company since 1979, is highly successful in competitive field archery with six National, three European and one World title to her credit. Her sport is very different from the better-known target archery as this is always done outdoors, usually in woodland, on slopes and in difficult terrain.

place during the year when the Research Workshop at Wincanton was closed and moved to the Sparkford site. Paul Buckland was now the sole trained mechanic, working in conjunction with the manual authors, who had the added responsiblity of taking their own photographs, following the practice adopted by their American counterparts.

Poor trading conditions still persisted in the US and Canadian markets, both of which were extremely competitive. Even so, the US trading companies turned in a very solid performance. Profit before tax increased by 58 per cent in US dollars, partly due to the ocean freight-related savings resulting from the decision to print US manuals in the USA. When printing in the USA commenced, the three web presses installed at Sparkford could be reduced to two. The two that remained were then combined into a single unit so that 32-page sections could be printed rather than the previous 16-page sections, speeding up output, especially on the bindery line.

The next financial year, 1992/93, showed sustained improvement in the Group's cash position, with record profits representing a 67 per cent increase on 1992. This was 28 per cent more than the previous record set in 1990. The Group had now generated enough cash to repay all its borrowings, while shareholder's funds had risen by 31 per cent. These and other factors confirmed that the Group was being successful in regaining its strong financial position, its employees performing better, having more information at their disposal, and a better opportunity to participate in its running. The success of the strategy to concentrate on the workshop manuals, the Group's core product, had been reflected in the end-of-year results. They had improved to such an extent that investment in capital projects could be re-

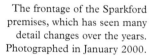

The frontage of the Sparkford premises, which has seen many detail changes over the years. Photographed in January 2000.

established and performance improved still further. Especially pleasing was the fact that these excellent results had been achieved not by a vast increase in sales but by the improved management of the business at all levels. Already, nearly £1 million had been spent in relocating and building a new Research Workshop and in reorganising the Motor Trade Editorial Department at Sparkford by equipping it with the latest desktop publishing technology – similar to that in use in the USA. Market research studies were now in hand to evaluate customer requirements in both the UK and the USA, to help develop the existing product range and to assess new opportunities.

As part of the commitment to good corporate governance, Panton Corbett was elected to the Board on 1 March 1993 as a Non-Executive Director. As Singer & Friedlander's Managing Director he had been responsible for organising the successful flotation of the Group in 1979 with a full listing on the London Stock Exchange, and had known the company for 20 years. Eric Oakley, the President of the US business, was given the Group-wide responsibility for sales and marketing, and Scott Mauck, the US Vice-President of Editorial, accepted Group-wide editorial responsibility for the core production range. Jeff Clew, the Group's Executive Editorial Director, had taken early retirement during February 1991 to work as a freelance journalist and Pete Ward, the UK Editorial Director, had been forced to seek early retirement due to illness, prior to Scott Mauck's promotion. Another appointment made during March 1993 was that of Marketing Manager, David Keel joining the Group in this capacity. Workshop manuals have always been the Group's core product, but there was now a worrying hint of a decline in their sale largely because the latest generation of cars were much better built than their predecessors and less likely to develop faults. This potential drop in sales could be more than offset if those who previously had been hesitant to buy a manual could be persuaded to do so.

Work had already started on an extension to the Nashville warehouse for the installation of a print plant so that the Group would be responsible for its own printing in the USA. It was scheduled to be fully operational by November 1993 giving the Group its own manufacturing facilities on both sides of the Atlantic.

Colin Davies was appointed UK Finance Director on 1 February 1994. He had joined the company in October 1991 as Management Accountant having previously qualified as a chartered accountant with Price Waterhouse in Cardiff. On 16 August 1997, Colin married Dawn Harris, also from the Accounts Department, this being one of the very few 'in-house' weddings that has occurred at Haynes!

Recovery from the recession continued throughout the 1994 financial year, with Group profits rising by 27 per cent to £5 million and almost doubling the amount of money in the bank. This latter achievement was all the more meaningful as over £2 million had been spent on replacing plant and machinery, which included the installation of a new and more sophisticated bindery line at Sparkford.

The UK contract printing business was closed during December, having failed to make sufficient headway in an extremely competitive market. Sadly, this involved the loss of a further 25 employees, many of whom had been with the company for a long time. Fortunately, alternative employment was found for almost all of them by the Group's outplacement programme. The closure accounted for a write-off of £233,000.

During the latter half of the year, the UK company invested in its first national television advertising campaign to attract those less inclined to undertake their own maintenance and simple repairs. They needed to be convinced that a Haynes Manual would not only give them the confidence to carry out these tasks but more to the point, would save them a considerable amount of money. Centred around the theme 'See Haynes, See How' the award-winning campaign kicked off with a 60-second slot on ITV before being put out on Channel 4 and satellite TV. The exposure was lengthened on bank holiday weekends. It was backed up by new 'waterfall' point of sale display stands in retail outlets in which a mass of covers full-on provided a strong and eye-catching attraction.

To fill the gap caused by the departure of Jim Scott during 1992, Keith Fullman took over the reins as the UK Managing Director in July 1994, combining this with his role as the Group's Financial Director. This gave Max Pearce better opportunity to concentrate on the overall management and development of the Group. For the first time in several years both the UK and the US economies benefited from low inflation, low interest rates, and stable foreign exchange rates, recovery in the USA having taken place much earlier than it did in the UK. While a period of steady growth for the year ahead could be forecast with some confidence, there remained one area of concern. Raw material prices were expected to rise considerably during the year, which would necessitate a constant review of production methods if good levels of profitability were to be sustained. Although there was now a considerable amount of optimism in both the UK and the US retail markets, as yet there was no discernible evidence of this in the UK automotive aftermarket, despite new car sales being well up on the previous year.

In the year ended 31 May 1995 the Group's pre-tax profits were £5.2 million compared with the £5 million generated the previous year. The year-end cash balance rose from £3 million to £3.5 million over the same period and included £220,000 profit from the sale of the Leeds warehouse. Particularly poor UK trading conditions during the first quarter of the year had not recovered by the year's end. In consequence, the increase in pre-tax profits had been achieved by the strength of the US business. Two thirds of the Group's income was now being generated from outside the UK, which underlined the importance of translating the manuals into foreign languages in a bid to help make the Haynes Publishing Group PLC a truly international company.

The newly released manuals in Spanish were expected to have good prospects when sold across the United States, Mexico and South America.

The sale of automotive manuals in France continued to grow, sales volumes having doubled by the end of 1995. It led to the formation that year of Editions Haynes, in Paris, a subsidiary company responsible only for sales, marketing and the distribution of the French language car manuals. The importance of this side of the business was acknowledged in August 1995 when Graham Cook was appointed Overseas Development Manager

A fall in UK operating profits due to poor manual sales was attributed to the demand for automotive DIY products being exceptionally weak. The introduction of an additional product range – the *TechBook* series – successfully helped to offset this. They were designed to complement the

Max Pearce, John Haynes and Keith Fullman.

The Book Trade Division, now the Special Interest Publishing Division, has had many high-profile book launches to promote new titles. John Haynes, with author Martin Bennett (left), who flew over specially from Australia for the occasion, pose with *Rolls-Royce and Bentley: The Crewe Years*, in the Rolls-Royce and Bentley London showrooms in Conduit Street. On the right is Chris Woodwark, then MD of Rolls-Royce Motorcars Ltd.   *(Peter Nicholson)*

'Somewhere over the North Sea' . . . the launch of a book about RAF Brize Norton air base was marked by the RAF laying on a VC10 flight which took members of staff and invited journalists over the North Sea including in-flight refuelling, for both passengers and aircraft. Years later, one well-known book trade journalist, who receives a book launch invitation most days of the week, declared this was the most memorable event he had attended! Left to right: Carole Turk, Karen Ley and Tony Kemp.   *(Peter Nicholson)*

Well-known local author, Derek Phillips of Yeovil, signs his latest railway title for OPC, *The Salisbury to Exeter Line*, for Roger Baker, the Mayor of Yeovil, watched by Mo Siewcharran (Marketing Manager), October 1997.
(Peter Nicholson)

workshop manuals by covering more general topics such as automotive electrical and electronic systems, and brakes.

Book fairs have played a vital role in making contact with existing and new customers, as well as providing the opportunity to push the sale of foreign book rights. These include the London and Frankfurt book fairs. Four people devoted to export sales and foreign rights were now employed in the UK, responsible for approximately 25 per cent of UK book trade business. By now the general publishing losses incurred in previous years had been eliminated through improved title selection and by capitalising more on current buyers' interests. The publication of a series of paperback titles on Formula 1 grand prix racing drivers was particularly successful.

Not to be underestimated is the value of selective book launches, two good examples of which were Ken Lawrence's *A Century of Cornhill Tests* launched at the Oval Cricket Ground on the day prior to a test match, and Michael Scott's *Wayne Rainey: His Own Story*, which was promoted at Donington, the track at which many Superbike events and motorcycle grands prix have been contested. This went on to become one of SIPD's most successful books ever.

Sales and profits in the USA were ahead of the previous year by 12 per cent and 19 per cent respectively, despite trading conditions continuing to be extremely competitive and research confirmed Haynes was now the clear market leader throughout North America. Raw material costs, especially for paper, continued to give cause for concern although steps had been taken to minimise the impact by advance purchases. Prevailing market conditions, however, prevented the company from passing these on by increases in cover price. Work to double the space of the warehouse and production plant in Tennessee was now in hand, for completion in late September 1995. This extension was needed to make provision for the increased storage of finished product as well as raw materials.

The Haynes stand at the Frankfurt Book Fair, October 1999, with Mark Broadley and Viktoria Tischer. *(Darryl Reach)*

It was particularly fitting that in the 35th year of the company's foundation its Chairman, John Haynes, achieved recognition for his services to publishing. He was appointed an Officer of the Order of the British Empire (OBE) in the Queen's 1995 Birthday Honours List, receiving the honour at Buckingham Palace from HRH The Prince of Wales, the following November. A proud day for all the family, who chastised John after the event for replying to Prince Charles's question of, 'Do you do a manual for my Aston Martin?' by saying, 'No', when he should have said: 'We will do one Sir, if you lend us your car, and you can have the first copy.'

When the results of the financial year ending 31 May 1996 were announced the Group could boast its best-ever pre-tax profit of £5.5 million.

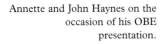

Annette and John Haynes on the occasion of his OBE presentation.

Furthermore, the US and the UK subsidiaries were able to report significant sterling increases in both turnover and profit. For the US this represented a continuation of their excellent performance over the last ten years and for the UK a welcome recovery in profitability after below par results in 1995. Sales in the UK and Europe of £12.5 million and profits of £1.5 million were ahead of the previous year by 16 per cent and 15 per cent respectively. This could be attributed to an improvement in sales of workshop manuals in the UK and in all products sold in overseas markets, especially Scandinavia and France. Sales volumes were showing substantial increases each successive year. To promote the sale of Swedish language titles launched during the year, Haynes Publishing Nordiska AB was set up in Uppsala, with the expectation of having a total of 25 Swedish language titles available by June 1998. Already this venture was proving to be highly successful. The possibility of titles in the Russian language was also under negotiation, to be produced in conjunction with a Finnish publisher. Ten titles, printed in the UK, were expected to be available by the end of 1998.

The cost of redesigning the workshop manuals, the translation of some titles into the Swedish language, and investment arising from the introduction of a range of home DIY books had a small but adverse effect on profit margins during the year. Raw material costs continued to be unpredictable. The redesign of the top-selling manuals and the purchase of the new 'waterfall' retail display racks mentioned earlier materially assisted the sale of workshop manuals in the UK and helped to offset this.

The Group continued to look for suitable acquisitions on either side of the Atlantic with which to enhance shareholder value. Regrettably, because of the intervention of the Federal Trade Commission, it had not been possible to reach an agreement to purchase the Chilton Book Company, the Group's major US competitor, after lengthy negotiations with Capital Cities/ABC. Against economic backgrounds of falling unemployment and interest rates in both the US and UK, some satisfaction could be derived from the fact that the inflationary environment was now benign. These economic trends

UK Sales Director George Magnus gets the wind in his hair as he is treated to a ride in a '£250 sports car'. The book describing how to make one of these cars has proved to be one of the Special Interest Publishing Division's best-ever selling titles. (Peter Nicholson)

combined with the changes taking place in the automotive aftermarkets around the world, were expected to give rise to significant rationalisation in future years. Already the separate wholesale and retail market sectors had begun to merge in the US as they had in the UK.

George Magnus rejoined the company on 12 August 1996 as the UK Sales Director. In the early days of the company he had joined as an employee of G. T. Foulis when it was acquired, but left later to become more closely involved with the automotive aftermarket. There had been many changes in the Sales Department during the intervening period and when he returned to head the department he brought with him a great deal of valuable experience of the aftermarket.

For the fifth consecutive year the Group was able to announce improved profits before tax. For the year ended 31 May 1997 these had risen to £5.6 million, with an end of year cash balance of £4.1 million compared with £2.8 million in 1996. The US business also achieved another noteworthy performance by continuing to increase dollar turnover, profits and market share. Unfortunately, both the UK and US businesses were now suffering from the effects of a strong pound, which reduced Group profits by £224,000. This was attributable to the translation of overseas earnings and assets into sterling and was not reflected in the cash flows. The cash balance at the end of the year was slightly higher than in previous years, reflecting the strength of the Group and the focus on cash management. Poor trading conditions during the first and final quarters of the year, partly due to the UK General Election, also had their effect. Yet even when these adverse conditions were taken into account, profits from the UK and Europe were still reasonable.

Trading throughout the year had been mixed. The US company profits had held up well, considering the modest increase in dollar sales. US consumer spending had declined for three consecutive months during the first quarter of the year for the first time since 1981, influenced by bad weather. With over two-thirds of the Group's turnover and profits being generated outside the UK, the negative impact of an unfavourable exchange rate had become noticeable. However, since the majority of Group profits were being earned in the United States, the decision to print the majority of the US manuals in Nashville, Tennessee, gave protection against the worst of the currency movements.

Sales of the Spanish language manuals in the USA, introduced the previous year, had more than doubled. Since the full extent of the anticipated increase in paper prices had not materialised this, together with longer print runs to help offset price rises, had resulted in lower unit costs and higher profit margins. Co-operation with a Japanese publisher had led to the availability of manuals, produced and printed at Sparkford, in the Japanese language covering the Mini and the Citroën BX series. The *Diesel Service TechBook* was available in Polish through a co-edition arrangement with Wydawnictwo Auto, and five Superbike manuals in German, printed at Sparkford, through a rights agreement with a

German publisher. Three more were to be available by the end of 1999.

Discussions about manuals in Chinese were in hand relating to VW and Citroën translations although progress had been hampered as this is a very price-sensitive area. This also applied to South Africa, although in this case the exchange rate of the rand and political unrest have created similar problems. India as yet remains largely unexplored.

Despite new capital expenditure of $2.4 million, mostly in connection with a new colour press, the US year-end cash flow had improved considerably. Plans for the coming year included placing an order for a second web press to keep the projected increase in output on target.

In the UK and Europe turnover had remained static, while operating profits had fallen by 10 per cent. Apart from the uncertain trading conditions mentioned earlier, many customers were focused on margin enhancement rather than the heavy price discounting that had characterised the market for some time. While this change initially had a negative impact on volume sales, it was expected to have a beneficial effect on profitability in the future. Sales and market share both continued to increase in France now that the majority of hypermarkets and auto centres were stocking Haynes manuals. This also applied to Scandinavia, where Haynes was now the market leader. In July 1998 Graham Cook was appointed to the board of J. H. Haynes & Co as the Overseas Sales and Rights Director. Visiting customers and devising strategy is an important part of his activities, with Russia now one of the fastest expanding markets. The overall objective is to retain control of rights and to undertake the printing whenever possible.

Sales of general publishing titles had fallen slightly during the year, even though losses had been reduced. A downturn in the bicycle market across Europe had been reflected by a sharp fall in sales of the cycling titles in both the UK and France. It was counterbalanced in the UK by sales of the caravan range of manuals and camping guides. Overseas sales of the cycle and

For the first time, the general public had the opportunity of seeing what goes on in the Haynes factory at Sparkford when an open day was held on 19 February 1997. Many local people took advantage of this unique opportunity which was also the occasion of the launch of the book *Sparkford: Memories of the Past.* Author Jeff Clew signs another copy, while left, Wendy Harris keeps an eye on the 'takings'.
(Peter Nicholson)

home DIY titles had shown significant growth, to maintain total UK turnover at the expense of lower levels of profitability. The UK and Europe remained the area of business from which the greatest improvements in the year ahead were expected.

To have achieved an increase in profitability for seven successive years was no mean accomplishment and it was with great pleasure that John Haynes was able to report this in his Chairman's statement that prefaced the 1998 Annual Report and Accounts. Profit before tax had increased again by 9 per cent and turnover by 5 per cent, against a background of having to face up to increasing competition in the US market. Appalling weather in the UK had undermined manual sales during the all-important spring selling period and progress in overseas sales had been limited by the continued strength of the pound and higher domestic interest rates.

During May 1998 further rationalisation of non-core imprints took place when the Oxford Publishing Company was sold to Ian Allan Publishing. The once buoyant railway book market had declined markedly for a number of valid reasons and this action was taken in the expectation that this decline would continue. By this time the G. T. Foulis imprint had also been allowed to lapse. Many of the titles it published had become increasingly integrated with the core Haynes name and the time had come to make a clearer distinction. When eventually only the Patrick Stephens imprint was reserved for any non-core titles, the Special Interest Publishing Division became a more closely defined operation, rationalisation having given it a stronger sense of purpose.

In the USA, consumer confidence was at a record high, fuelled by strong income growth and job creation. An operating profit of $8.9 million represented a 3 per cent increase over the previous year after provision had been made for a substantial bad debt at the end of the year. Sales had increased by 7 per cent above the 1997 figure. Further increases in paper prices continued to be offset by additional efficiences in printing operations, to keep the gross profit percentage at the same level as the previous year. The second high-speed web press had been installed at Nashville during the fourth quarter of the financial year and was fully operational.

A highlight of the year had been the establishment during October 1997 of a new business in Australia with a range of Haynes Manuals that by March 1998 would cover approximately 80 per cent of indigenous cars on Australia's roads such as Holden and Ford. Located in a suburb of Melbourne it had been set up as a branch of Haynes Publications Inc, the US sales and distribution company, to operate out of a 7,000 square foot office and warehouse. The new range of manuals relating to Australian-manufactured vehicles had been originated in Melbourne during the previous seven months, where vehicles were stripped down and photographed so that the manuals could be presented in the traditional Haynes style. Sold through Australia's largest wholesale and retail parts group, they were available from their stores on a nationwide basis by early November 1997.

The Group now had a firm foothold in the Pacific Rim region.

The Australian operation had already made a small contribution to the net profit in this financial year and steady sales growth was projected for the future. Meanwhile the UK and European businesses achieved a small increase in turnover despite disappointing trading during the final quarter of the financial year. Although export turnover was still being affected by the strength of the pound, strong sales of the Group's four *Titanic* titles had been generated by James Cameron's film, aided by co-publishing agreements in the USA. One of these, *Titanic: Triumph and Tragedy*, appeared for a while in the *Sunday Times* best-sellers list. Overall, this was a remarkable achievement, bearing in mind that two of the books had first been published more than ten years earlier. This, and continued operational efficiences, led to an increase in profits to provide an unexpected bonus.

In the second half of the year the Group benefited from a gain of £160,000 by disposing of a colour press. This contrasted with a loss of £120,000 incurred when a press had been sold during the previous year. It was replaced in February 1998, and as a result, the Production Division was once again able to undertake its own high-quality colour print work in-house. The addition of a second web press to the US print line reduced the Group's cash position to £2.3 million. A review to assess what additional work would be required to ensure that there would be no undue disruption to its operations as a result of the 'Millennium bug', showed the total cost to make all the Group's critical business systems Year 2000 compliant, would not exceed £140,000. Although the UK would not be an initial member of the European Monetary Union, the opportunity was also taken to assess what existing and future impact a single currency would have on the Group to ensure that it was prepared for and could take advantage of monetary union if and when it came.

One interesting fact emerged from what had been a very difficult and challenging period. All the attention that had been given to recovering from the recession and then charting a path to successful recovery had masked the fact that the market itself had undergone significant change. Videos in particular had provided strong opposition to the conventional book due not only to their visual form of presentation but also to their ability to deliver fashionable 'sound bites'. Later, the increasing interest in computers took its toll too. Many leisure hours were spent surfing the Internet in preference to reading a book. The sale of railway books had tended to suffer most due to an additional factor, the dwindling number of the older generation to whom at one time a steam locomotive had been a part of everyday life. The younger generation had experience only of diesel and electric traction and were more in tune with videos, up-to-the-minute, all-colour glossy magazines and the Internet for much of their news and information.

Experience underlined the need not only to continue to be highly selective when commissioning new titles but also to take a fresh look at how books should be presented and packaged.

The beginnings of a diversification into manuals other than those that dealt specifically with cars and motorcycles can be traced back to the 1980s when a manual on domestic petrol-engined lawnmowers was published. It was an exploratory move to see whether it was possible to extend the range of DIY manuals into other areas, retaining the familiar 'strip and rebuild' sequence interspersed with numerous photographs. The format closely resembled that of the other workshop manuals, this being largely because the Production Department at that time was well-accustomed to their already long-established type of layout. Despite the fact that this 'breakaway' manual was seen as little more than a probe into an uncharted area, it was well received. On the strength of this a second manual was originated to complete the coverage of all the more common pedestrian-controlled rotary and cylinder mowers in use at that time.

As the market leader in workshop manuals it was evident that the association between Haynes and their characteristic DIY approach was now widely recognised, which encouraged thoughts about further new titles. The need for manuals covering the repair of household domestic appliances seemed an obvious requirement and a new series of titles was commissioned by the Book Trade Division (now SIPD) along these lines. Their coverage ranged from washing machines, dishwashers, washer driers and tumble driers to oil-fired central heating systems. These titles provided an opportunity to venture away from the more formal type of workshop manual presentation which could have had a restricting influence on sales to those who consider themselves not to be interested in things mechanical. It made them more user friendly, even though the same basic step-by-step strip and rebuild concept still largely applied. That they were well received is no understatement for such has been their success that many of the original titles are still in print, albeit updated.

In the early 1990s there was a marked turn towards protecting the environment, with an active lobby against the high levels of pollution created by the ever-increasing number of vehicles on the road. As a result the bicycle came back into fashion, not just for covering relatively short journeys but also as a means of keeping fit and providing a pleasant leisure-time pursuit for the family. The opportunity to exploit this situation presented itself during late 1992 when a group of people on the staff, including Kevin Hudson who abandoned his burgeoning career in the Accounts Department to edit it, David Keel, Matthew Minter, Paul Wells, Tony Kemp, David Notley and Kevin Perrett, got together to produce the first edition of *The Bike Book: everything you need to know to help you enjoy and maintain your bicycle*, by J. Stevenson. David Hermelin designed and made the pages of the book at home, while recovering from a broken leg! There seemed little doubt that the bicycle was set to come back into prominence due to an ever-growing interest in environmental issues, with sales likely to increase substantially as the 21st century drew closer. The publication of such a book could not have been better timed and, covering every aspect of the bicycle, its full-colour

Haynes has its own cricket team which plays regular friendly matches with customers, suppliers and other local companies in the summer months. During the 1999 season the side remained unbeaten in all matches played. This photograph shows a cheque for £500 being presented to a representative of CLIC (Cancer & Leukaemia in Children), a registered fund-raising charity. This followed a charity match in 1996 when the Haynes team played a Showbiz XI captained by Ian Hislop of *Private Eye* and *Have I Got News For You* fame.

The company has a well-equipped gymnasium at Sparkford available for all members of staff – an idea originating from the Innovations scheme.

presentation proved extremely popular. Fred Milson took over from the book's original author for the second and third editions. Sales far exceeded expectations and co-editions were subsequently published in a dozen languages with sales exceeding half a million worldwide.

The success of *The Bike Book* encouraged an extension into a series of books suggesting recommended bicycle rides in various parts of the country which would guide cyclists to some of the more scenic and traffic-free routes. All of the routes were specially selected to form the basis of a new *Ride Your Bike* series, with the books containing clear, numbered directions marked on Ordnance Survey Landranger mapping. Each was a spiral-bound paperback with approximately 120 colour illustrations and about 20 maps. To accompany the series the *London Cycle Guide* was published in May 1998, along with *My First Bike Book*, which was written for 5–8 year olds.

With ample evidence of such a high level of demand for other DIY books the Home and Leisure Division was formed to permit even deeper penetration into such hitherto-unexplored areas. Initially the newly formed division was headed by Nicholas Barnard, formerly an author for Dorling Kindersley, who already had experience in this field. His stay and that of two colleagues he had recruited to assist him was short-lived and the division was then taken under the wing of Alan Sperring, the UK's Production Director, who had been with the Group for 20 years.

One area that seemed to offer potential related to ways and means of improving the home. Because all Haynes Manuals are based on first-hand practical experience a special studio was built at Sparkford so that the correct techniques for wallpapering and decorating could be explained with accompanying photographs. Each book ran to 96 pages and contained full-colour illustrations. At the time of writing there are six titles in the *Home Decorating* series which cover topics ranging from painting, tiling, and wallpapering to stencils and stencilling. They are accompanied by a further five books in the *Home Soft Furnishing* series, which are guides to aid the selection of cushions, curtains and blinds as well as the design of bedrooms and bathrooms. Appropriately, the theme 'learning from experience' runs throughout all the home DIY titles.

As had been the case with *The Bike Book,* co-editions provided an important avenue for the *Decorate Your Home* series, adding to their widespread appeal and making them a very popular and profitable venture. They can now be found in languages as diverse as Swedish, Spanish and Polish. The creation of all these new titles underlined the need to revive in revised paperback format some of the earlier publications about domestic appliances. These were kept in print and re-packaged to form the *Budget Series*. In 1999, three of these titles ran to further new editions, reverting to their original hardback format, with others following in 2000.

Caravan and camping enthusiasts have been catered for by a series of *Good Camps Guides*. Produced with Clive and Lois Edwards of Deneway Guides and Travel Ltd, the first titles under the Haynes imprint became

available in January 1997 listing caravan and camping sites in Europe, France, and Britain and Ireland, all of which are regularly visited by the authors to ensure high standards are maintained. Adequately indexed for ease of reference they also contain maps and discount vouchers for ferry travel, caravan and motor caravan insurance, and selected campsites. The guides make a valuable addition to the successful *Caravan Manual* by John Wickersham and *The Complete Caravan Book* by Ally Watson. Since then, a further title has been added to this growing list – John Wickersham's *The Motorcaravan Manual* – with *The Trailer Manual* published in early 2000.

Towards the end of 1999, Mark Hughes, former Editor of *Autosport* and *Classic and Sports Car* magazines joined the Sparkford staff. Initially, his role was to take responsibility for the Home and Leisure Division, but additional tasks include working with Darryl Reach on the commissioning of new car and motorsport titles for the Special Interest Publishing Division. It was also intended that he would oversee the merging of the two divisions prior to Darryl semi-retiring in Autumn 2000.

It was announced in early March 2000 that Haynes Publishing Group PLC had reached agreement with the Channel Islands-based newspaper publisher, Guiton Group Ltd, to acquire from them Sutton Publishing Ltd, the Stroud-based publisher of history books. This £4 million acquisition will give Haynes a broader based business in the United Kingdom, lowering the dependence on manuals, and more fully utilising the printing and distribution facilities based in Somerset. The resultant printing of Sutton titles at Sparkford will also help to counterbalance the effect of transferring printing and binding of UK car and motorcycle manuals to the US plant from mid-2000.

10

The introduction of new technology

Towards the end of the 1980 financial year, the company lost production of something like 150,000 books creating an imbalance of stock levels, due to several weeks of industrial action by the National Graphical Association. The issue at stake was the introduction of new technology. The union had no disagreement with the company, the strike having been brought about by the use of 'on-screen' electronic page make-up by the national newspapers based in London. It had been adopted by the newspaper proprietors to supersede the traditional typesetting and paste-up operations such as those deployed at Sparkford. The changed working practices based on more sophisticated computer-based techniques represented a significant saving in time, but also meant a reduction in staffing levels and a requirement for the operators to have a hitherto unknown degree of flexibility. Eventually it had to be acknowledged that progress could not be ignored and after a long and bitter struggle the Union's acceptance of new technology was agreed.

Ian Mauger joined the Group on 14 April 1986 as Analyst Programmer. Until his appointment David Haynes had previously held responsibility for the administrative computer systems in his capacity as the Group's Finance Director and Company Secretary. It took Ian 18 months to analyse the company's systems and involve all departments in the specification of a new MV9500 system and new application software, to make access more available to senior management. At the start of this period, management accounts were completed off-line using the new Apple II personal computers, later to be replaced by IBM compatible PCs. The new system replaced the old Data General Nova, which had fulfilled primarily a business support role. Its main function, other than to provide very basic business information composed mainly of sales data, had been to process orders and maintain both the sales ledger and the control of stock. It gave access to eight users and had a link to the Leeds warehouse. An inherent problem lay in tracing customer orders once they had been entered as there was no real-time stock control in the sense that it was not possible to tell exactly at what stage a customer's order was until the goods had been despatched. The solution was to install a completely new system using software from ECMS and a financial suite from

Mega. This latter company provided the project management and ECMS staff were available on site for 24 hours a day for three weeks during the system's installation and commissioning, as was Ian himself. It was a period of frantic activity which often meant nights sleeping on the floor.

There was also need to retrain the operators of the old system, Rita Hill and Sally Strelley, both long-serving employees. This was carried out on site by the ECMS and Mega staff. After the first 18 months the Data Processing Department was formed, with Ian in charge. A first programmer was also appointed, Andy Pook, who had been recruited from Plymouth Polytechnic and trained by Ian. As time progressed Joanne Greenage, Andy Youngs and Julie Winzar were taken on by the Department, the last replacing Sally Strelley who had left to start a family.

When Mega went bankrupt the financial suite had to be replaced with software from Strata, which had its source code written in Powerhouse. In due course the name of the Department was changed to that of Management Information Services, by which time Mandy Warry, Mike Churchill and Geraldine Herd had also joined the team. Their appointments made a great difference to the way in which paperwork circulated throughout the Group. Previously orders had been taken by telephone and entered on order forms, whereas they could now be fed directly into the computer.

A new costing system was also devised by Kevin Hudson, a graduate from Cambridge University, and this represented a considerable step forward. Working with Andy Youngs he was able to maintain better control of stock levels. Books were now categorised by an 'A' to 'F' coding to denote the rate of sales off-take of each individual title. When this was in place it was possible to carry out a viability check on projected new titles, based on sales of similar books and estimates provided by the sales force.

Computers were now about to be introduced to the UK editorial staff. A much earlier investigation into the use of word processors by the Editorial Department had been started by Jeff Clew and Mansur Darlington. Appalled by the archaic way in which the manuscripts originated by the car and motorcycle manual authors were being submitted in longhand they knew something had to be done, even if none of the authors had any keyboard experience. Since Jeff was one of the few members of the Editorial Department who could use a typewriter competently, albeit with the time-honoured 'two-finger stab' of a journalist, he enrolled for an IBM computer course in Bristol. This served not only as a good introduction to word processors but also revealed how easy it would be to adapt to them, and what reduction in time could be achieved by originating a manuscript in this manner. This last factor would also have to take into account the time required to train users from scratch. Once this information had become available Jeff and Mansur visited several equipment suppliers to assess what was best suited for the application in mind and to obtain an idea what it would cost to purchase and install a suitable system. Unfortunately pressure of work and more urgent priorities meant the survey had had to be abandoned before any firm recommendations could be made. Now Ian Mauger had the opportunity to take matters that vital stage further and submit his own proposals.

Initially, a system using word processors of Amstrad manufacture was installed but unfortunately this was short-lived as it proved unreliable after 18 months service and had to be replaced by more dependable Olivetti equipment. A valuable addition to the staff was Annie Toomey, who brought with her considerable experience of book and magazine publishing from London. Her arrival had a significant impact on the Data Processing Department where her strong personality and organisational abilities were soon evident. Not only did she establish PC procedures and practices but also trained staff, some of whom had no previous computer experience. She spent some 12 months setting up an ambitious forward programme which sadly came to a premature end when she was tragically killed in a motor accident. Her loss was felt throughout the entire Group.

The interior of the Sparkford warehouse showing the fork lift truck method of operation.

On 6 July 1990 Ian Mauger was appointed Information Technology Director of the UK business in recognition of the substantial contributions he was making to the availability of vital management information. Those who had benefited most were the sales office and warehouse/distribution. Later, when Ian's title was changed to Operations Director, he took on additional responsibilities that included control of the Sparkford warehouse. The installation of a new picking line during 1994 enabled orders to be selected by zone and the cartons moved on a conveyor system. Until now this task had been labour intensive, with the need to move trolleys from place to place as each order was made up. Now the same number of books could be got ready for despatch by only half the staff, which sadly resulted in some redundancies.

One problem still persisted with the despatch of orders to customers. Whenever a large consignment of cartons was delivered the customer had no means of identifying which one contained a much-needed book without having to unpack them all. By writing a packing module for the computer software the problem was overcome. It helped not only to reduce the number of cartons but also produced the much-needed identification labels to show the content of each box. A bar code on the label gave the carton's weight, to obviate the need for any physical checking.

During 1994, Customer Services also came under Ian's control, which helped significantly to integrate the whole process of order handling and matching stock levels to demand, thereby improving customer relations. The telephone system was uprated, both internally and externally, so that an enquirer would not feel they had been cut-off if a query had to be passed to someone else within the company before a full and satisfactory answer could be given.

After Camway Autographics, which later became known as the Design Department, had moved into their new purpose-adapted building in October 1990 a burning question that needed to be addressed was the adoption of new technology. They had been using a database running initially on an Olivetti PC and later an AppleMac, to maintain all the title information needed to produce the Haynes Publishing World Catalogue twice a year. As previously stated, word processors had then still to be introduced to the Editorial Department and experience with Camway's own AppleMac equipment had been impressive. This had shown that when page design was carried out on screen four people could handle what would have required 12 previously without this equipment. A detailed report was submitted to the Main Board by David Hermelin and Alan Sperring to show how considerable and long-lasting economies could be achieved. When Haynes Publications Inc went ahead and adopted a similar AppleMac system, Sparkford's Motor Trade Editorial Department followed suit.

Another technological advance of note was the installation of an ISDN (International Standard Data Network) line, to enable the high-speed transfer of digital files. Almost all scanned images are now received by ISDN and an increasing number of advertisements are sent to magazines by the same route.

The new CtP (Computer to Plate) installation at Sparkford, which enables book pages on disk to be imposed and transferred direct to a printing plate without the need for intermediary film.

Often, an advertisement will not exist physically until it appears in the magazine – a significant advance from the traditional paste-up of artwork.

A reduction in the advertising budget encouraged in-house printing and other efficiences to give rise to a 'doing more with less' situation. Spin-offs included the design and implementation of a catalogue on CD-ROM which was ultimately to be used to form the basis of a fully functional web site and the production of leaflets for direct mail shots. Short-run colour posters have also proved economically viable by using a direct film-to-plate colour printing facility.

Although only briefly mentioned in connection with its pioneering use of AppleMac computers, the Design Department designs virtually everything apart from the content of most books. Its work has included upgrading the layout and cover design of the car and motorcycle manuals, and jacket designs for the Special Interest Publishing Division's books. With the dramatic increase in overseas activities members of the Design Department (in conjunction with many other departments) now often find themselves working in a variety of different languages. Proofreading has in consequence taken on an entirely new dimension!

The Design Department's largest role is that of sales support, working hand in hand with the Marketing Department, with whom they share the same building. By far the biggest job is the compilation of the annual complete catalogue, now published each September and which currently lists some 1,600 titles. It takes one person the best part of three months to collate all the material for inclusion in each issue through the need to list ever more information. This includes the Haynes product code, the ISBN (International Standard Book Number) and the recommended retail price for each and every title, manuals included. All this is over and above other relevant information such as the author's name, a brief description of the book's content, its size, number of pages and number of illustrations. A New Titles Supplement to the main catalogue is published in March.

Few areas have undergone such a fundamental change in such a short period of time as book design and production. Barely ten years before, Camway Autographics had been struggling with its first word processor, an old Olivetti with a dot matrix printer. Not one of the staff was computer literate. Today they sit at a multi-thousand pound work station, proficient in numerous software programmes. They can electronically retouch photographs, typeset, paginate, manage complex data bases, prepare and administer equally complex colour output, and occasionally design things! Gone are the days of separate specialist copywriters, creative designers, typesetters and finished artists etc.

In December 1999, Haynes Publishing installed at Sparkford a Scitex Lotem platesetter system with digital proofing to enable digital information to be transferred direct from computer to printing plate – the computer-to-plate system (CtP).

Previously, disks were sent to the USA for output through the imagesetter at Nashville, Tennessee, and the imposed film was then supplied to Sparkford for printing.

The Heidelberg Speedmaster 102 five-colour press on which a major proportion of SIPD titles and book covers are printed.

11

The changing face of the Haynes Manual

Those who have purchased Haynes *Service and Repair Manuals* over the years cannot fail to have noticed how their style and format have changed, even though the original concept has never altered. If a manual is to be really useful there is no substitute for stripping and rebuilding a car or a motorcycle, photographing each sequence of the operation, and accompanying the photographs and line drawings with step-by-step instructions provided by the author. Not only can attention be drawn to parts that may be difficult to remove or replace without risk of damage but also details can be given of how to do so without the need for special service tools unless they are absolutely essential. Cost saving is obviously an important consideration in view of the high labour charges when repairs or overhauls are carried out by a garage. Furthermore there is also a warm sense of inner satisfaction in knowing that by following in the steps of the expert, the job has been well done.

The very early manuals were paperbacks, later to be replaced by padded plastic covers with a line drawing on the front and pages that were affixed by what was then referred to optimistically as perfect binding. Perfect it wasn't after much use and it was not unusual for a customer to phone in and start off by saying 'I have got one of your loose leaf manuals...!' Soon the car manuals changed to a stout card cover and had pages no longer in danger of working loose. The motorcycle manuals had a soft cover from their introduction in 1973, similar in design to that of the car manuals, although it was not long before a colour photograph of one of the machines covered replaced the line drawing, which boosted sales. Unexpectedly, this change in cover design gave rise to problems when motorcycle manuals were sold in the USA. Because the American imported models had different colour schemes (and sometimes model names) customers were reluctant to purchase a manual that showed a UK imported model on its cover. If a US specification machine was featured, the same sales resistance was evident in the UK. At that time it was not feasible for each market to have its own printed cover, even though the content was identical, but when printing commenced in Nashville this problem was overcome. For some reason, the car manuals had always been subject to heavy discounting by retail outlets, whereas the UK motorcycle market had not been subjected to this.

The greatest danger in producing manuals is complacency. Just because the existing manual range is selling well does not mean there is no room for improvement. Lessons are constantly being learnt and customer comment is an excellent way of monitoring whether the objectives of a manual are being achieved. From time to time regular market surveys have been carried out, either by inserting a card in each manual to request the user's comments, or by using the services of an independent market research company. Customer suggestions have always been taken into account if they were practicable, to help create an even better product. But there were always some that could not be accommodated for valid reasons, of which the following are a few random examples.

The question has been asked many times if spanner sizes can be included in the text which, taken at face value, is by no means an unreasonable request. However, this is an area fraught with danger as it is not unknown for manufacturers to change the size of nuts and bolts or similar fasteners without prior notification. Some do not even mention it in their regular service bulletins to their agents and dealers which, in any case, can often be difficult to obtain from outside the dealer network. On the occasions when spanner sizes had been mentioned in the past, it gave rise to problems and often needless frustration. Those who went out and purchased a special size of ring spanner or socket to complete a particular job were not amused when it did not fit. Some even went so far as to claim a refund for whatever tool they had bought in vain as that size had been given in the manual!

Much the same applied to left-hand threads, the bane of the car and motorcycle worlds that seemed to catch out quite a few. It is not unknown for a manufacturer to change from a right-hand to a left-hand thread, or vice-versa, without prior warning. While the author will have advised in his text where these difficult threads are likely to be encountered, they were just as likely to be caught out in the same way if these changes had been made after the manual had been written. What is surprising is how many adopt a brute force and ignorance approach when a fastener is difficult to move in the conventional direction, even if 'LH' is clearly stamped on it. Inevitably extensive damage results – and another bill is put in the post to Haynes Publishing!

A lot of these problems are caused by dismantling or rebuilding in the incorrect sequence. There is a great deal of truth in the old saying 'whenever all is lost, consult the manual!'. By then, of course, it is usually too late. Needless to say much correspondence has been received from customers who had queries of various kinds or required further detail about dismantling or reassembly procedures that were causing them problems. These often requested a reply by return and were greatly outnumbered by telephone calls demanding even more urgent action. The need to maintain a telephone answering service with quick reference to archive material became imperative, even if many of these enquiries arose simply because the text in a manual had not been read correctly or had even been completely ignored. Everyone received a courteous reply, even the 'professional complainers' or those who were rude to the switchboard operator. The answers were provided by the authors, who much preferred to do so in writing. Constant interruptions to answer telephone enquiries often meant it would be necessary to hunt through archive material, which would completely disorganise that person's working day. Eventually a system was set up whereby the calls would be answered by the person in charge of the archive material, who would be responsible for recording the details and relaying back the answer.

The suggestion has been made on occasion that a manual should be more educational in content or deal with a specific area such as the carburettor, electrical system or fuel injection in much more detail. Without significantly expanding the size of the manual (and increasing its cover price) the only alternative was to publish a series of manuals to deal specifically with these areas. Electrical systems have always been the area to generate most enquiries, usually because wiring diagrams are difficult to follow or interpret with any confidence. This is where the Group's computer-aided design system came into its own in 1991. It was then possible to reduce the number of wiring diagrams in a manual by about two thirds, to the user's advantage. In motorcycle manuals colour wiring diagrams had been originated on the CAD system since 1997, with considerable savings over the earlier hand-originated colour diagrams. The books giving greater detail on a number of specific subjects rapidly grew in number and were quite separate from those produced for the garage trade, some for use by the UK market and others for the USA.

A Montego is completely stripped down for photography in the Research Workshop at Wincanton, October 1987.

Eventually they became part of what is now known as the *TechBook* series, all of them being system rather than model orientated. Their main asset is that they are able to cover both the theoretical and practical aspects of a vehicle system in more detail than can be expected in a workshop manual. The *TechBook* title was adopted because this range of books has considerable additional potential in schools, technical colleges and universities.

The most commonly asked question is, 'why does it take so long to originate a new car or motorcycle manual when so many of the vehicles are on the road?'. The answer to this is two-fold. First, although about 95 per cent of a manual could be originated without any problems it is necessary also to include the various running clearances, bearing tolerances and wiring diagrams before the manual can be completed. These can be obtained only when they are available in published form, a delay that can often prove frustrating. Furthermore, it is also necessary to obtain up to date sales figures from the Society of Motor Manufacturers and Traders (SMMT) in the case of cars, or from the Motor Cycle Industry Association (MCIA) in the case of motorcycles, to ensure there is a sufficiently good market to make a new title economically viable. Even these figures can sometimes prove misleading, and it is necessary to consider other factors such as overseas sales and customer demand to support the case for originating a new manual. It is an acknowledged fact that a manual is rarely passed on when a car or motorcycle is sold, so each sale tends to generate another manual purchase. In this instance the number of manuals likely to be sold could be at the least doubled, and possibly even trebled, to give a completely different picture.

Market research has shown on many occasions that only a relatively small number of customers purchase a manual because they intend to carry out a major repair or overhaul. This is all too apparent when requests for a manual covering an entirely new model are received within a matter of days of its launch. Most buy a manual to have a readily available reference source to consult should a query arise, or just to have an idea of the complexity of their car or motorcycle. As mentioned earlier, others make good use of the routine maintenance section to save themselves money, and in the event of a fault developing can make some assessment of the problem to avoid being 'ripped off' by an unscrupulous repairman. Many purchase a Haynes *Service and Repair Manual* whenever they buy another car or motorcycle simply by force of habit. They need no convincing of its usefulness.

By the 1980s the manuals had become considerably refined, with much clearer photographs and line drawings through the application of modern technology in their production. In 1988 Pete Ward decided to take a look at changing the style of the text in the car manuals in liaison with Perkins, the diesel engine manufacturers. They had developed what they termed 'Perkins approved clear English', with the objective of making their own manuals more user friendly when English was not the reader's mother tongue. No firm conclusions were reached largely because other areas aimed at simplifying a manual's content also needed to be considered. This situation was later addressed by a series of *Technical Dictionaries* supplied on a free-of-charge basis to overseas purchasers of manuals. They are currently available in 16 different languages, with more in preparation. Covering all the technical part names and terms used in the average manual they have become increasingly popular with non-English-speaking mechanics throughout Europe and the rest of the world.

When the control of the Motor Trade Editorial Department was transferred to the USA under Scott Mauck, an interchange of staff from the US and UK Editorial Departments followed. This was so that each could obtain a better appreciation of the other's working practices, with a view to harmonising them as far as was practicable. Already the motorcycle manuals had adopted the American practice of providing a much-enlarged section on trouble-shooting at the rear of the book and the more detailed routine maintenance schedules at the front. Only very brief details had been given in the earlier manuals under the belief that to have given such information would have been seen as 'preaching to the converted'. It had not been appreciated that some bought a manual for the routine maintenance section only, because they considered it to be the one part they could handle with competence if they were not mechanically minded. Once they had gained confidence they would often be encouraged to progress to more ambitious repairs and it was this important factor that needed to be taken into account.

JJ Haynes, John and Annette's eldest son, joined the company on 3 February 1992 as a graduate trainee having obtained his BA (Hons) degree in business studies at Brookes University, Oxford. After at first working with the US company he returned to the UK to work at Sparkford, to take an interest in product development. As the manual format had remained substantially unchanged for some considerable time he suggested the presentation of the content might be too formal and make assumptions about a user's depth of knowledge. After discussions it was agreed that the objective should be not just to make a manual more user friendly but also to effect economies to offset rising production costs.

Further market research brought to light some important facts. The main criticism was a need to change the text-to-illustration balance so that many more photographs could be included. Long, wordy text procedures were disliked. It also appeared that very few users ever stripped and rebuilt a gearbox so, by dispensing with this section, a reduction in the number of pages could be achieved. That this was the right decision there can be no doubt, as very few protests were received from any dissatisfied purchasers after the gearbox section had been omitted.

What was also discovered was that the detailed cutaway drawing on the front of each car manual (long regarded as a Haynes 'hallmark') would often deter potential purchasers as it gave the impression the book was highly technical in content. Substituting a less detailed cutaway would conveniently provide further economies while achieving the desired effect without substantially changing the appearance of a manual. The original very detailed cutaway drawings, mostly originated by Terry Davey, had always proved time-consuming and expensive to originate. The improved cover design also brought a change of title for the series to cater for a changing market. The long-familiar *Owners Workshop Manual* is now the Haynes *Service and Repair Manual*.

Input from the US company acted very much as a catalyst at this time and by 1995 the text in both the car and the motorcycle manuals produced in the UK and the US had been changed in accord with American recommendations. The text was now set in three columns, contained fewer line drawings but more photographs, and had shorter paragraphs. An indication of the skill level required for the various procedures was also included.

All these changes made a manual much easier to use, while at the same time effecting significant production economies without impairing the Group's reputation for the quality of its product. There was now a more marked similarity between the US and the UK manuals, although they could never be made identical due to differing requirements in the two respective markets.

An interesting issue arose during one of the company's strategic planning meetings. All Haynes Manuals were sold under a common pricing policy, one price for the car manuals and another for the motorcycle titles. It was queried whether it would now be appropriate to change this policy with regard to the motorcycle titles. Because the original motorcycle manufacturers' instruction books and similar publications were no longer available on the older machines of British manufacture or for the early Japanese models, there seemed to be adequate scope for keeping in print the Haynes Manuals covering these models. Although the demand might not be as high as that for the newer manuals, there was a growing trend to find and restore the older models which in turn would make the older titles an invaluable source of reference. To keep them in print would mean smaller and

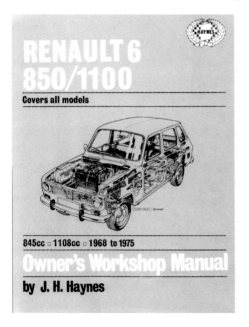

The changing face of the Haynes Manual.

hence more costly print runs, in which case a two-tier price structure would be feasible, the 'classic' manuals having a higher cover price. It would also help compensate for the fall-off in the origination of new titles due to the continuing decline in the UK and US motorcycle markets at that time. This suggestion was implemented and differential pricing came into being during 1991. With the passage of time it permitted a third category of motorcycle manual to be introduced to coincide with the new generation of Superbikes. The range of three and four-cylinder Hinckley Triumphs presented an ideal subject for their launch in early 1996. These, too, merited a higher cover price.

When the US motorcycle market began to improve, a joint venture was entered into with the US company in 1992 to originate only new motorcycle titles that would be suitable for both that market and the UK. Eric Oakley, the President of the US company, was given the responsibility for reinvigorating the then dormant US motorcycle manual market and Scott Mauck with implementing the origination of the new titles. As the USA still had the larger of these two motorcycle markets, the manuals were written there, with some input from the UK. The situation was eased somewhat by the employment of a former Clymer managing editor, Alan Ahlstrand, who worked from his home. The manuals he originated were the first to feature the revised text/illustration balance and were well received by the trade, who saw them as a commitment to the production of a new range of titles.

During 1993/94 the origination of new motorcycle titles continued to meet the requirements of both markets, but from 1995 onwards, different marketing requirements necessitated the separation of interests. The emphasis in the UK was now on Superbikes, whereas in the USA it was ATVs (all terrain vehicles) and off-road models that assumed prominence. Superbike titles were distinguished by their eye-catching covers featuring colour photographs of various versions of the models concerned on the front, and action shots on the rear.

The Superbike manuals introduced in 1996 carried over the improvements made by the US Editorial team, plus the new page layout developed for the car manuals, but also included new information on the MoT test, winter storage, advice on the use of tools, a four-page model history. A hard backed cover improved durability. Development of these manuals has continued with the introduction of colour wiring diagrams and key colour sections in the text.

The drive to increase car manual sales had also been materially aided by the changes in content and presentation to make them more user friendly. Furthermore, to make it apparent that Haynes was the market leader and intended to remain so by keeping abreast of current technological advances, a manual on the Ford Mondeo was made in CD-ROM form for demonstration purposes. Also now available was a CD-ROM version of the *Automotive Technical Data Book*. The adoption of this form of presentation overcomes all the inconvenience of ready access to a video while the repair work is actually in progress. Not only is it possible to print out all the sections that need to be followed during the dismantling and examination operations, but also the list of requirements to ensure the job can be completed satisfactorily without interruption.

Translation rights for manuals continue to bring in useful additional income as mentioned earlier. An arrangement was entered into during 1997 with a German co-publisher, Delius Klasing, for the German translation of three of the new Superbike motorcycle titles that had recently been published.

Some have queried whether Haynes Manuals are likely to be of less use these days as the latest generation of cars are equipped with engine management systems which are beyond the scope of most DIY enthusiasts when faults develop. This is an area to which considerable thought had already been given, to the extent that a Haynes Professional Fault Code Reader was launched in 1998. Designed to interrogate engine management systems, this simple to use hand-held diagnostic tool is capable of reading and resetting fault codes. It was aimed at the UK garage trade as an entry level product and supplied with a comprehensive end-user support package. A few months later the usefulness of the diagnostic tool was aided by the publication of the *Automotive Diagnostic Fault Code TechBook*. Containing tables of diagnostic fault codes related to engine management systems in typical Haynes fashion, it shows how they can sometimes be extracted by improvised means, using the fault code reader if necessary.

The high incidence of accidents amongst young motorcyclists has been a matter of concern for a long time, a problem of which the Haynes Publishing Group was well aware. Their desire to help reduce the number of road accidents led to their sponsorship of the late Dave Taylor's nationwide motorcycle road safety campaign, aimed at teenage motorcyclists. His infamous non-stop 'wheelie' around the 37¾ mile TT course in the Isle of

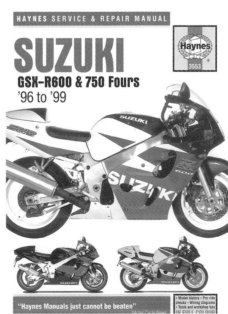

Evolution of the Haynes motorcycle manual.

Man, may have seemed at variance with these objectives but anyone who attended one of his road safety talks could not fail to have been impressed. His role in helping to bring about a significant reduction in the number of accidents amongst young motorcyclists was officially recognised by the award of an MBE. It is unfortunate that his campaign was cut short when he finally succumbed to cancer.

The 25th anniversary of the publication of the first three motorcycle *Owners Workshop Manuals* occurred in 1998, a fact commented upon at that year's UK International Motor Cycle Show. Their author, Jeff Clew, went on to originate the first ten titles in ten months and eventually 19 in total and held the record for originating an urgently needed title from scratch after an author had defaulted. It took him exactly ten working days to complete, working from only the photographs. Of his original three motorcycle manuals the one relating to the BSA Bantam is still in print, virtually unaltered.

Sponsorship has also been used to good advantage to create a wider awareness of both the company and its products. When the company agreed to sponsor a four-stroke motocross championship in 1976 after the original sponsors had withdrawn, it was reinvigorated as the Haynes Four-Stroke Championship. Its sponsorship under the Haynes banner created a tremendous amount of goodwill and it continued to be supported for the next 20 years during which it generated many column inches, and often full page spreads, in the motorcycling press. It was by no means uncommon for the father of a rider who participated in the championship series to call at the Haynes stand at a trade show and express his appreciation of the company's support. More recently, Haynes has sponsored an amateur motor racing championship run by the 750 Motor Club for home-built sports cars, following on from the highly successful publication of Ron Champion's *Build Your Own Sports Car for as Little as £250.*

A company day out was organised in August 1997 for the World Superbike Championship round at Brands Hatch, together with trade hospitality for key customers. Haynes was sponsoring rider James Whitham (in shorts), seen here with Haynes staff.

12

The Haynes Motor Museum

Having founded a flourishing book publishing business with cars and motorcycles as its root, and participated in motorsport events at club level, it was inevitable that John Haynes should give thought to building up a representative collection of the cars that appealed to him most, and so he started to acquire cars in the late 1960s.

Even in the early days, he had an eye for a good machine and in 1969 bought a 1959 Jaguar XK150 drophead. Although not quite a classic at the time, John realised its potential and still owns and enjoys that very same car which has been on rallies all over the UK and Europe and even to the North Cape! John Haynes's first vintage car was a 1930 six-cylinder Morris Oxford. It must have seen better days as on his way home with his new acquisition he had to get to the top of a very steep hill in the time-honoured way of ascending in reverse to benefit from the lower gear ratio! Other cars soon followed including an impressive 1949 Jaguar 3½-litre saloon sporting a bonnet which seemed to go on to infinity, and a 1963 Daimler SP250 Dart with its glassfibre body. There was also a 1934 Austin Seven saloon, just to remind him of his first book on building Austin Seven Specials which was to shape his destiny as a publisher.

In no time at all the collection grew and storage began to become a problem. All manner of buildings were used, many of them borrowed from friends, as well as the old stables at the Haynes Publishing Group site at Sparkford. It was, however, a far from ideal situation as the vehicles could not be stored in suitable conditions to prevent deterioration, nor could they be restored in buildings with such restricted access. The effects of condensation began to take their toll so that the only satisfactory solution to the problem was to acquire or have built a large building where the collection could be housed together. The obvious answer was to set up a museum, assuming a convenient building could be found or existing buildings extended. Not only would it keep the collection together in a much more hospitable environment but also it could provide the opportunity for the vehicles to be maintained and, if necessary, restored to their former glory. They could also be seen by car enthusiasts who would provide entrance revenue to help reduce overheads.

The opportunity to pursue the latter course of action presented itself when part of the site at the sawmills complex in Sparkford became available, mostly rough ground that during the Second World War had served as an ammunition dump. About half a mile from the Haynes Publishing factory, it was ideally located, lying between the single-track railway line from Castle Cary to Weymouth and the A359. This road joins the A303 which runs between the museum and the Group's Sparkford headquarters and is the main holiday route to the West Country. Even since the A303 was upgraded to by-pass Sparkford village it is still only a minor detour to visit the museum. At the time of opening the nucleus of the collection comprised a total of 29 vehicles including three motorcycles. Mike Penn was taken on as the museum's Curator to help shape it.

Further lateral thinking and a growing desire to put something back to benefit other enthusiasts, many of whom had probably bought Haynes Manuals and other books over the years, led to the careful consideration of making the museum into an independent charitable trust. So, in 1985 the collection was awarded charitable trust status which provided certain advantages, not least of which ensured that the collection belonged to the 'Nation' and could not be split up, a fate that had befallen other collections in the past. It also meant John had to relinquish ownership of his vehicles and he claims it took him a whole week before he could bring himself to put his

An aerial view of the museum site as it was at the time of opening in 1985.

signature on that vital piece of paper! He retained only six cars as his own personal possessions, which included his favourite, a bona fide 1965 4.7-litre V8 AC Cobra 'muscle' car.

Although the museum bore no allegiance to the publishing business other than through its founder, the Haynes family interest was represented on the board of trustees, with John as its Chairman.

Initially, the original single-storey building which had served as office accommodation on that part of the sawmills site was pressed into use, with Jane Pean as its first receptionist. The reception area later included a book shop which stocked Haynes workshop manuals and a large selection of general books, including those of other publishers, all with a transport flavour. The floor area that lay immediately behind contained the cars and motorcycles, which gradually came closer together as the collection grew. Additions were now being sought selectively at auctions or acquired through other means such as private transactions.

As an aside, Mike Penn had an unusual problem after the museum had opened. He was regularly dragged out of bed from his home several miles away at 4 o'clock in the morning when the security alarms were set off. It always happened on a Monday, which suggested that something repetitive was happening to trigger the tamper alarms. As the railway ran close to the back of the museum it occurred to him that it might in some way be responsible, and on making enquiries through British Rail, he found a goods train heavily loaded with Portland stone passed along the line at exactly the time and day when the alarms went off. The heavy vibrations it created were sufficient to activate them, so it was only a question of having their sensitivity adjusted to be sure of an unbroken night's sleep in future.

The Sparkford Motor Museum, as it was then called, opened quietly, with only a typed list of exhibits available to the local press. The official opening took place on 10 July 1985 by Richard Noble, the then holder of the World Land Speed Record. This he had achieved by driving his jet-engined car *Thrust 2* at 633.468mph (1,019.25kph) in the Black Rock Desert, USA. A party was held on the site that evening to celebrate the company's 25th Anniversary which ended with a brilliant fireworks display.

The formal opening of the museum attracted a great deal of interest from the media and by now more of the mass-produced cars that were once a familiar sight on our roads were being added to the collection. These included examples such as a 1954 Austin A40 Somerset and a 1966 Ford Anglia 105E, with which visitors could identify and have fond recollections of what might well have been their first car. Perhaps understandably, nostalgia seemed to concentrate more on the early post-war cars, although the more exotic and the very early models that represented Britain's motoring heritage also attracted much attention.

An especially appealing aspect of the collection is that it was never intended to be a museum in which its vehicles were only ever static exhibits. Fully restored externally, there was no possibility of using their outward appearance to hide worn-out or incomplete engines, sagging suspension, or bodywork which had filler to obscure rust or other defects. Every car that came into the museum had to be in virtual concours condition, or if it was not, capable of being restored to this standard and to its original specification before it went on display. Absolute authenticity was the all-prevailing factor.

The opening of what eventually was to become Hall 5 by the museum's Curator, Mike Penn, on 14 April 1987 added a storeroom extension and made possible the addition of a growing collection of American cars. Some served as a reminder of the 'prohibition' era of the gangsters, and the later 'gas guzzlers' with their powerful engines and sometimes bizarre styling. Many had never been seen before other than perhaps on the cinema screen by those who had not ventured across the Atlantic.

Outside the museum a 1km tarmac track was laid so that the cars could be demonstrated during 'open days', with facilities for tests of driving skills. It had been anticipated the track would also be used for just a few days each year for either kart racing or sprints, after the RAC had certified it and conducted noise monitoring tests with sound meters. Indeed, during one of the test days, when karts were circulating, a chain saw in use at a neighbouring farm registered a much higher decibel reading! Sadly, after only a few well-supervised events had been run, a handful of local residents complained bitterly to South Somerset District Council about the noise and even the smells created by the castor-based racing oils! Some of these complaints originated from outlying areas so far away from the site that noise, let alone smells, could not possibly have been detected under even the most unusual circumstances. The council clamped down and issued a 'desist forthwith'

Richard Noble OBE, right, and John Haynes at the opening of the museum in 1985.

warning, banning all future events of a competitive nature with the threat of legal action if they did not cease. Fortunately, the ban did not apply to driving tests and track demonstrations on 'open days', which were able to continue as originally intended.

It was soon necessary to add Hall 3, a further sizeable extension to the museum and it was fortuitous that the visiting Governor of the State of Tennessee, Ned McWherter, was able to lay the foundation stone on 4 July 1988. He had been visiting the factory at Sparkford to commemorate the opening of the new 36,000 square foot warehouse in Nashville. Appropriately it was American Independence Day and he presented John Haynes with a personalised number plate issued by the State of Tennessee.

The new hall was officially opened less than one year later on 24 April 1989, the 21st birthday of Marc Haynes who was then appointed to the Board of Trustees and later went on to become the museum's Managing Director with a BSc Honours Degree in business studies from Manchester University.

Hall 3 had a 12,000 square foot floor area, making it possible at last to house all the International Collection encompassing cars from countries such as Japan, Russia and India, ranging from a Baja three-wheel rickshaw to a Lincoln Continental and including a number of what today are referred to as microcars, rather than the earlier and more descriptive 'bubble cars'.

Provision was made for a cafeteria at the top end of the museum, immediately to the rear of the reception area, which proved a popular facility for those who wished to make the most of their visit to the museum – and for those who worked there!

Now the museum had a small but highly skilled workforce who not

Ned McWherter, Governor of the State of Tennessee, unveiling the foundation stone for the new museum extension, 4 July 1988.

John Haynes is presented with a personalised registration plate from Tennessee. Ned McWherter and David Suter on the right.

only maintained and restored the vehicles in the museum but were able to undertake similar work on behalf of customers. A key member of the restoration team was Ron Warne, a genius in the art of restoration and highly proficient at renovating bodywork in the traditional way of filling and reshaping with lead. Sadly, his death in February 1995 left quite a void in the team although his legacy remains in the high quality of the restoration work he had already carried out. A simulated period vehicle workshop, 'Ron Warne's Smithy', was later built and dedicated to him at the far end of Hall 1's 'Dawn of Motoring' display.

Later, the workshop team gained the responsibility for maintaining the Group's fleet of cars and commercial vehicles. Meanwhile, Mike Penn was building up a comprehensive collection of archive material with which to research the authenticity of future acquisitions and to provide an information service in response to the growing number of enquiries received from car enthusiasts.

The collection continued to grow in size and one of the next moves was

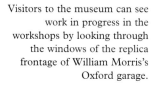

Visitors to the museum can see work in progress in the workshops by looking through the windows of the replica frontage of William Morris's Oxford garage.

to transform the storeroom into Hall 5, in which cars would be restored. It enabled visitors to see for themselves the work going on through windows in its frontage, which was a carefully reconstructed replica of William Morris's original garage in Oxford. The hall was officially opened on 8 April 1992 by Roy Madelin, Chairman of South Somerset District Council and the Rt Hon Mrs Jennifer Vickers, the Mayor of Yeovil. The British car collection was rearranged so that it could be positioned in front of the Morris Garage to display to advantage vehicles such as a Bullnose Morris Cowley and one of the two prototype Rover estate cars. As Halls 4 and 5 were adjoining, the British and American car collections could be brought into close proximity with each other.

By this time the museum was hosting events organised by one-make car and motorcycle clubs, and similar organisations. The hospitality offered to those fortunate enough to receive invitations to the opening of the new extensions, and the facilities now available on site, aided the promotion of the conference and training facilities available for corporate hire. The museum was now in a position to stage its own events, aimed primarily at classic car enthusiasts. These began with the resurrection of the Haynes Classic Tour as a 2½-day event organised by the RAC Motor Sports Association and were followed by others including the Haynes Spring Classic in which enthusiasts were able to experience first-hand the disciplines of motorsport, the end-of-season Autumn Leaves Classic Tour, and a Treasure Hunt on Boxing Day, ending with a supper.

Car hire for weddings has become another feature, usually involving the use of the 1971 Rolls-Royce Corniche with its registration number ERO 54 which looks suspiciously like EROS 4! Wedding receptions can be held in the museum with a civil marriage conducted amongst the cars following the change in the law in recent years.

In late 1993, a further small extension was opened, to be followed by a big breakthrough not long afterwards when one of the two-storey sawmill

The museum's 1971 Rolls-Royce Corniche, ERO 54 is in much demand for weddings. The bride on this occasion was Book Trade Editorial Secretary, Jane Fear, in July 1990.
(Peter Nicholson)

The museum also houses conference and hospitality facilities.

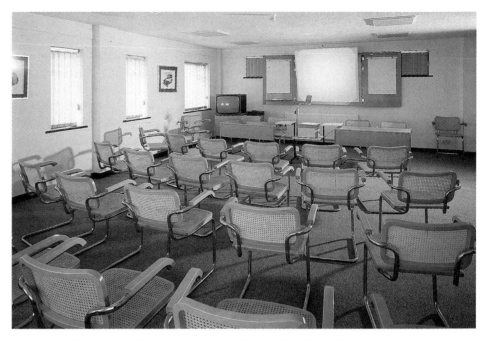

product display buildings and its immediately adjoining land became available. The cafeteria was transferred to what was originally the bookshop with the reception area, and the bookshop-cum-reception area moved to the ground floor of the new building after it had been substantially remodelled. By this time, the bookshop was expanded to sell models and model kits, posters, souvenirs, and museum orientated casual wear.

The museum's administrative offices were relocated to the upper floor of this building. The linking of the new building with the main body of the original museum created even more display space and provides visitors with an introduction to the 'Dawn of Motoring' display in Hall 1 which they pass through on their way to Hall 2. Once inside this hall, they are greeted by the 'Red Collection', an amazing assembly of red sports and GT cars. This display takes into account all tastes, from a rare 1951 six-cylinder Turner sports car to a 1981 Lamborghini Countach, not forgetting John Haynes's own AC Cobra. These two halls were officially opened on 11 July 1995 by Murray Walker OBE, the well-known Formula 1 commentator who did so in his own inimitable style.

The centrepiece and the most valuable car in the museum, which many consider to be the most beautiful of vintage cars, is the Duesenberg Model J with just 471 supremely engineered chassis made between 1928 and 1937. Only eight Derham-bodied Toursters were produced and this one is the only example that can be seen outside the USA. They were clothed in the finest bodywork that money could buy.

It may be six decades since the last Duesenberg left the company's Indianapolis factory, but you'll still hear Americans exclaim, 'It's a Duesey!' when describing something outstanding. The Model J, the mutual

masterpiece of engineer Fred Duesenberg and the go-getting boss of the Auburn-Cord Duesenberg Corporation, Errett Lobban Cord, brought the marque immortality.

This mighty 6,816cc twin-cam straight-eight luxury car was launched at the December 1928 New York Automobile Salon to a chorus of superlatives. Fast, powerful and massively built, it was good for around 120mph with open bodywork, 140mph when fitted with a centrifugal supercharger, and even the open Sport Phaeton on the 'short' (11ft 11in) wheelbase chassis scaled 2.4 tons. The Model J cost $8,500 in chassis form. Admittedly, in those days you got nearly nine dollars to the pound, but you could still have bought 40 brand-new Model A Fords for the price of a single Duesey.

In America, however, even in the darkest days of the Great Depression, there was a glittering elite that could afford the very best, and Hollywood in particular loved the Duesey. Owners included Gary Cooper, Clark Gable, Tyrone Power, James Cagney, Greta Garbo, Joe E. Brown, Mae West and Howard Hughes. William Randolph Hearst and his mistress Marion Davies both owned Duesenbergs.

This particular dark and pale blue two-tone car was owned by Otis Chandler, the publisher of the *Los Angeles Times*, so it is especially appropriate that it passed into the possession of John Haynes OBE. Its passage to the museum from New Jersey via air freight to Paris was entrusted to Mike Penn, who can give a vivid account of all the problems he had to overcome when he refused to be parted from this $1 million car at any stage of the long journey and which formed the basis of an article in the *Sunday Telegraph* dated 26 June 1994. Positioned at the far end of Hall 6, the Tourster takes pride of place on

The museum's centrepiece – the Model J Derham-bodied Tourster Duesenberg on its revolving platform.

a slowly revolving turntable to the musical strains of Gershwin's 'Rhapsody in Blue'. It is also a very popular inclusion in photographs taken when wedding ceremonies are held on a red carpet in front of it at the museum.

The museum was honoured by the presence of the legendary racing driver, Sir Stirling Moss, who opened Hall 8, the most recent extension, the 'Hall of Motorsport', on 11 June 1997. Thus dedicated, it reflected the general ethos of the museum by having on display a collection of racing cars and motorcycles representing the golden years of motorsport from racing at club level to Formula 1. An unusual feature is the devotion of a section to a race accident that took place at Thruxton Circuit a year earlier involving a Porsche 911. Fortunately, no-one had been injured and it has been used with accompanying story boards to show in a non-sensational way the important role played by race marshalls and trackside safety precautions. A background race track mural is made even more effective by the sound of racing cars passing by at speed.

Part of the display includes John Haynes's third racing car, an Elva Courier, which he campaigned with some success in the 1960s. John had always regretted selling his Elva so it became something of a challenge for Curator Mike Penn to relocate it. This he did by writing to the DVLC with the tale that he was writing a book on sports cars and needed to locate this particular example which had the registration number 27 ALO. It was found in a very sad and poor state and required extensive restoration, but enough of it remained for Annette Haynes to recognise the Perspex side windows she had made all those years before and the original gold cellulose paint. Annette decided to present John with the restored car as a Christmas present. To avoid discovery by John and thus spoiling the surprise, the Elva had to be located and restored away from the museum. During the subsequent five-month restoration many hours were spent away from the museum by the mechanics particularly the chief mechanic at that time, Simon Taylor. This did not go unnoticed by John whose suspicions were aroused by the number of occasions his key staff were missing and things nearly came to a head just before Christmas when Simon's further employment at the museum was placed in doubt because of the long periods of absence. Of course, all was well when John discovered the real reason that his staff were missing, when Annette presented him with his Christmas present, duly tied up with a large red and yellow bow. The mechanics however vowed they would never do it again as it was far too dangerous and stressful!

Little has so far been said about the motorcycle exhibits, mostly located between the cars wherever there is space available. Amongst them can be found a small section devoted entirely to speedway racing, with a display of programmes from many of the provincial tracks that have long since ceased to exist. There are also some colourful riders' jackets, one of which is a rare

Motorcycle history is also well represented at the Haynes Motor Museum. These four speedway bikes were restored by Jeff Clew.

John Haynes's third racing car, the Elva Courier – rescued from scrap condition many years later and restored by museum staff on behalf of Annette Haynes who presented it to her husband as a Christmas present. Now on display in pristine condition in the Hall of Motor Sport.

example from the long-closed but now reopened Workington track. With them are four speedway bikes, one of which is almost certainly the only survivor still in running order out of 22 Velocette 415cc dirt track models made during 1929. This project started with nothing more than an authentic 1929 engine bearing the KDT engine number prefix and it took a further 20 years or so to source all the other parts before a complete machine could be built. The display also serves as a poignant reminder of the era when the JAP speedway engine dominated world speedway racing.

An essential part of any museum is its catalogue, its quality being particularly important to the visitor. The first catalogue was originated by Jeff Clew, when he was working for the museum for a brief period in 1991. It ran

On some occasions, cars are taken around the museum's 1km test track. John and Marc Haynes admire the beautifully restored 1917 Morris Cowley 'Bullnose' as it is put through its paces.
(Peter Nicholson)

to 24 pages and was compatible with the size of the museum at the time. Being a 100 per cent motorcycle enthusiast, Jeff was glad to make use of Mike Penn's collection of archive material to be doubly sure the detail about the cars was factually correct.

As the museum grew in size, the catalogue was updated to keep pace and the second edition ran to 48 pages with numerous illustrations. The third and current edition is even more impressive. It contains an eight-page colour section, 25 pages of black and white illustrations and has been expanded to a total of 72 pages.

The strong educational role played by the museum is borne out by the number of school children who visit it, usually in pre-arranged groups accompanied by teachers. They are invited to take part in a questionnaire type competition in which the answers can be found by careful observation of the vehicles on display. Some find the video cinema, with its tiered seating, like a free visit to the cinema, although it is by no means the province of children alone. It is located in Hall 3 and has a continuously running programme. If need be, it can double as an auditorium for product launches and training sessions.

John and Annette's youngest son Christopher is the latest member of the management team to lend his expertise. Chris studied leisure activities at Loughborough University and puts his not inconsiderable skills to good use in organising the many events and promoting conference and training facilities which are available for corporate hire. Chris is responsible for all types of corporate entertainment at the museum from army tank driving days to major product launches which all help to support and run the museum collection. One of Chris's success stories has been the creation of the Haynes Motor Museum Enthusiasts Association on a subscription basis by introducing a VIP membership card. This allows the holder unlimited free admission and entitlement to bring up to five guests per visit at the discount rate reserved for large parties. It also provides admission to the exclusive Association days held several times a year. Appropriately the association's free newsletter, to which all members are entitled, is *The Duesey*.

Today, the museum ranks high on the list of Somerset's major visitor attractions and is conveniently close to the Fleet Air Arm Museum at Yeovilton. Facilities exist for a joint visit to both at a reduced rate of admission, to form the basis of a full and memorable day out for the family.

Although the museum is an independent registered charitable trust, as mentioned earlier, and has no direct connection with its founder's publishing business, it could not have been foreseen during its evolution just how much spin-off it would have to the benefit of the latter. It has helped attract new business, triggered off long and lasting business relationships and inspired many personal friendships. Above all else, it has emphasised the deep-rooted devotion to the internal combustion engine with which the Haynes name has become synonymous, both in the world of transportation and in leisure time, as a source of relaxation and sheer pleasure.

Haynes titles in print, January 2000

750 Racer *Peter Herbert in association with Dick Harvey*

Action Stations 10: Supplement and Index *Bruce Quarrie*

Action Stations 8 (2nd Edition) *Bruce Barrymore Halpenny*

Action Stations Overseas *Sqn Ldr Tony Fairbairn*

Acura Integra & Legend (86 - 90)

Acura Integra & Legend (90 - 95)

Air Accident Investigation *David Owen*

Air Band Radio Handbook (6th Edition) *David J. Smith*

Alan Rogers' France: Rented accommodation on quality sites

Alan Rogers' Good Camps Guide - All Year Round 1998

Alan Rogers' Good Camps Guide - Britain and Ireland 2000

Alan Rogers' Good Camps Guide - Europe 2000

Alan Rogers' Good Camps Guide - France 2000

Alfa Romeo Alfasud/Sprint (74 - 88) up to F

Alfa Romeo Alfetta (73 - 87) up to E

Alfa Romeo: Haynes Classic Makes Series *David Owen*

Alvis (3rd Edition) *Kenneth Day*

AMC Alliance & Encore (83 - 87)

AMC Mid-size models (70 - 83)

Archie and the Listers *Robert Edwards*

Aston Martin & Lagonda (4th Edition) *Chris Harvey*

Aston Martin: Haynes Classic Makes Series *Robert Edwards*

ATV Basics

Audi 100 & A6 Petrol & Diesel (May 91 - May 97) H to P

Audi 100 (Oct 82 - 90) up to H & 200 (Feb 84 - Oct 89) A to G

Audi 4000 (80 - 87)

Audi 5000 (77 - 83)

Audi 5000 (84 - 88)

Audi 80 (72 - Feb 79) up to T

Audi 80, 90 (79 - Oct 86) up to D & Coupé (81 - Nov 88) up to F

Audi 80, 90 (Oct 86 - 90) D to H & Coupé (Nov 88 - 90) F to H

Audi Quattro Book, The *Dave Pollard*

Austin Seven Source Book, The *Bryan Purves*

Austin Seven *Chris Harvey*

Austin/MG Metro (80 - May 90) up to G

Austin/MG/Rover Maestro 1.3 & 1.6 (83 - 95) up to M

Austin/MG/Rover Montego 2.0 (84 - 95) A to M

Austin/Rover 2.0 litre Diesel Engine (86 - 93) C to L

Austin/Rover Montego 1.3 & 1.6 (84 - 94) A to L

Automotive Body Repair & Painting Manual

Automotive Brake Manual

Automotive Carburettor Manual

Automotive Computer Codes

Automotive Diagnostic Fault Codes Manual

Automotive Diesel Engine Service Guide

Automotive Disc Brake Manual

Automotive Electrical and Electronic Systems Manual

Automotive Electrical Manual

Automotive Emission Control Manual

Automotive Engine Management and Fuel Injection Systems Manual

Automotive Fuel Injection Systems *Jan P. Norbye*

Automotive Gearbox Overhaul Manual

Automotive Heating & Air Conditioning Manual

Automotive Service Summaries Manual

Automotive Timing Belts Manual - Austin/Rover

Automotive Timing Belts Manual - Ford

Automotive Timing Belts Manual - Peugeot/Citroën

Automotive Timing Belts Manual - Vauxhall/Opel

Automotive Welding Manual

Ballooning *Anthony Smith and Mark Wagner*

Bedford CF (69 - 87) up to E

Bedford/Vauxhall Rascal & Suzuki Supercarry (86 - Oct 94) C to M

Beetle, The (2nd Edition) *Hans-Rudiger Etzold*

Benetton: Formula 1 racing team *Alan Henry*

Berger, Gerhard (2nd Edition) *Christopher Hilton*

Bike Book, The (3rd Edition) *Fred Milson*

BMC/BL Competitions Department, The *Bill Price*

BMW 1602 & 2002 (59 - 77)

BMW 2-valve Twins (70 - 96)

BMW 3- & 5-Series (sohc) (81 - 91) up to J

Dishwasher Manual *Graham Dixon*
Dodge & Plymouth Neon (95 - 98)
Dodge & Plymouth Vans (71 - 96)
Dodge Aries & Plymouth Reliant
   (81 - 89)
Dodge Caravan, Plymouth Voyager
   & Chrysler Town & Country
   Mini-Vans (84 - 95)
Dodge Challenger & Plymouth
   Sapporo (78 - 83)
Dodge Colt & Plymouth Champ
   (78 - 87)
Dodge Dakota Pick-up & Durango (97
   - 99)
Dodge Dakota Pick-ups (87 - 96)
Dodge Dart & Plymouth Valiant
   (67 - 76)
Dodge Daytona & Chrysler Laser
   (84 - 89)
Dodge Omni & Plymouth Horizon
   (78 - 90)
Dodge Pick-ups (74 - 93)
Dodge Ram 50/D50 Pick-up & Raider
   and Plymouth Arrow Pick-up
   (79 - 93)
Dodge Shadow & Plymouth Sundance
   and Duster (87 - 94)
Dodge Spirit & Plymouth Acclaim
   (89 - 95)
Dodge/Plymouth/Chrysler Rear-wheel
   drive (71 - 89)
Drawing and Painting Racing Cars
   Michael Turner
Ducati 600, 750 & 900 2-valve V-Twins
   (91 - 96)
Ducati: 50 golden years
Duckham's Story, The *Robin Wager*
E Type: End of an Era (2nd Edition)
   Chris Harvey
Eighth Air Force Bomber Stories
   Ian McLachlan & Russell J. Zorn
Electrical Appliances *Graham Dixon*
Escort Mks 1, 2, 3 & 4
   Jeremy Walton
Ferrari 1947-1997
   Edited by Gianni Cancellieri
Ferrari: Formula 1 racing team
   David Tremayne
Ferrari: The battle for revival
   Alan Henry
Fiat 124 Sport Coupe & Spider
   (68 - 78)
Fiat 500 (57 - 73) up to M

Fiat Cinquecento (93 - 98) K to R
Fiat Panda (81 - 95) up to M
Fiat Punto Petrol & Diesel
   (94 - Oct 99) L to V
Fiat Regata (84 - 88) A to F
Fiat Tipo (88 - 91) E to J
Fiat Uno (83 - 95) up to M
Fiat X1/9 (74 - 89) up to G
Fifty Years of Ferrari *Alan Henry*
Final Flights *Ian McLachlan*
Fix Your Bike
Ford & Mercury Full-size (75 - 87)
Ford & Mercury Mid-size (75 - 86)
Ford 1.6 & 1.8 litre Diesel Engine
   (84 - 96) A to N
Ford 2.1, 2.3 & 2.5 litre Diesel Engine
   (77 - 90) up to H
Ford Aerostar Mini-vans (86 - 96)
Ford and McRae *Derick Allsop*
Ford Automatic Transmission Overhaul
   Manual
Ford Capri II (& III) 1.6 & 2.0
   (74 - 87) up to E
Ford Capri II (& III) 2.8 & 3.0
   (74 - 87) up to E
Ford Contour & Mercury Mystique (95
   - 98)
Ford Cortina Mk IV (& V) 1.6 & 2.0
   (76 - 83) up to A
Ford Courier Pick-up (72 - 82)
Ford Crown Victoria/Mercury Grand
   Marquis (88 - 96)
Ford Engine Overhaul Manual
Ford Escort & Mercury Lynx (81 - 90)
Ford Escort & Mercury Tracer
   (91 - 96)
Ford Escort & Orion (Sept 90 - 97)
   H to P
Ford Escort (75 - Aug 80) up to V
Ford Escort (Sept 80 - Sept 90)
   up to H
Ford Escort Mk II Mexico, RS 1600
   & RS 2000 (75 - 80) up to W
Ford Explorer & Mazda Navajo
   (91 - 98)
Ford Fairmont & Mercury Zephyr
   (78 - 83)
Ford Festiva & Aspire (88 - 97)
Ford Fiesta (76 - Aug 83) up to Y
Ford Fiesta (Aug 83 - Feb 89) A to F
Ford Fiesta (Feb 89 - Oct 95) F to N
Ford Fiesta Petrol & Diesel
   (Oct 95 - 97) N to R

Ford Granada & Mercury Monarch
   (75 - 80)
Ford Granada & Scorpio
   (Mar 85 - 94) B to M
Ford Granada (Sept 77 - Feb 85)
   up to B
Ford Ka (96 - 99) P to T
Ford Mondeo Diesel (93 - 96) L to N
Ford Mondeo Petrol (93 - 99) K to T
Ford Mustang & Mercury Capri
   (79 - 93)
Ford Mustang (94 - 98)
Ford Mustang II (74 - 78)
Ford Mustang V8 (July 64 - 73)
Ford Orion (83 - Sept 90) up to H
Ford Pick-ups & Bronco (73 - 79)
Ford Pick-ups & Bronco (80 - 96)
Ford Pick-ups & Expedition (97 - 98)
Ford Pinto & Mercury Bobcat
   (75 - 80)
Ford Probe (89 - 92)
Ford Ranger & Bronco II (83 - 93)
Ford Ranger Pick-ups (93 - 97)
Ford Sierra 4 cyl. (82 - 93) up to K
Ford Sierra V6 (82 - 91) up to J
Ford Taurus & Mercury Sable
   (86 - 95)
Ford Taurus & Mercury Sable
   (96 - 98)
Ford Tempo & Mercury Topaz
   (84 - 94)
Ford Thunderbird & Mercury Cougar
   (83 - 88)
Ford Thunderbird & Mercury Cougar
   (89 - 97)
Ford Transit Diesel (Feb 86 - 99)
   C to T
Ford Transit Petrol (Mk 2)
   (78 - Jan 86) up to C
Ford Transit Petrol (Mk 3)
   (Feb 86 - 89) C to G
Ford Vans (69 - 91)
Ford Vans (92 - 95)
Ford Windstar (95 - 98)
Four-Stroke Performance Tuning
   (2nd Edition) *A. Graham Bell*
Freight Rover Sherpa (74 - 87)
   up to E
French Sports Car Revolution, The
   Anthony Blight
Fuel Injection Manual (86 - 96)
Garden Railway Manual, The
   C. J. Freezer

General Motors Automatic
Transmission Overhaul Manual
General Motors Buick Century,
Chevrolet Celebrity, Oldsmobile
Ciera, Cutlass Cruiser & Pontiac
6000 (82 - 96)
General Motors Buick Regal, Chevrolet
Lumina, Olds Cutlass Supreme &
Pontiac Grand Prix (88 - 95)
General Motors Buick Skyhawk,
Cadillac Cimarron, Chevrolet
Cavalier, Oldsmobile Firenza &
Pontiac J-2000 & Sunbird (82 - 94)
General Motors Buick Skylark &
Somerset, Oldsmobile Achieva &
Calais, and Pontiac Grand Am
(85 - 95)
General Motors Buick Skylark,
Chevrolet Citation, Oldsmobile
Omega & Pontiac Phoenix (80 - 85)
General Motors Cadillac Eldorado,
Seville, Deville, Buick Riviera &
Oldsmobile Toronado (86 - 93)
General Motors Cadillac Eldorado,
Seville, Oldsmobile Toronado &
Buick Riviera (71 - 85)
General Motors Chevrolet Cavalier
& Pontiac Sunfire (95 - 98)
General Motors Chevrolet Lumina
APV, Oldsmobile Silhouette &
Pontiac Trans Sport (90 - 95)
Geo Storm (90 - 93)
GM and Ford Diesel Engine Repair
Manual
Great Passenger Ships of the World
Today *Arnold Kludas*
Harley-Davidson Big Twins (70 - 99)
Harley-Davidson Sportsters (70 - 99)
Heinz-Harald Frentzen
Christopher Hilton
High Cold War *Robert Jackson*
Hillman Avenger (70 - 82) up to Y
Hitler's Grands Prix In England
Christopher Hilton
Holley Carburetor Manual
Home DIY Repair and Renovation
John Wickersham
Home Plumbing *Derek Johnson*
Home Security
Sonia Aarons & Donna Gilbert
Honda Accord (76 - Feb 84) up to A
Honda Accord (84 - 89)
Honda Accord (90 - 93)

Honda Accord (94 - 97)
Honda Accord (98 - 99)
Honda ATC70, 90, 110, 185 & 200
(71 - 85)
Honda C50, C70 & C90 (67 - 99)
Honda CB/CD125T & CM125C Twins
(77 - 88)
Honda CB100N & CB125N
(78 - 86)
Honda CB250 & CB400N Super
Dreams (78 - 84)
Honda CB400 & CB550 Fours
(73 - 77)
Honda CB650 sohc Fours (78 - 84)
Honda CB750 & CB900 dohc Fours
(78 - 84)
Honda CB750 sohc Four (69 - 79)
Honda CBR400RR Fours (88 - 99)
Honda CBR600F1 & 1000F Fours
(87 - 96)
Honda CBR600F2 & F3 Fours
(91 - 98)
Honda CBR900RR FireBlade
(92 - 99)
Honda CBX550 Four (82 - 86)
Honda CD/CM185 200T & CM250C
2-valve Twins (77 - 85)
Honda CG125 (76 - 94)
Honda Civic & Acura Integra
(94 - 98)
Honda Civic (84 - 91)
Honda Civic (Feb 84 - Oct 87)
A to E
Honda Civic (Nov 91 - 96) J to N
Honda Civic 1200 (73 - 79)
Honda Civic 1300 & 1500 CVCC
(80 - 83)
Honda Civic 1500 CVCC (75 - 79)
Honda Civic and del Sol (92 - 95)
Honda CR250R & CR500R
(86 - 97)
Honda CR80R & CR125R (86 - 97)
Honda CX/GL500 & 650 V-Twins
(78 - 86)
Honda Elsinore 250 (73 - 75)
Honda GL1000 Gold Wing (75 - 79)
Honda GL1100 Gold Wing (79 - 81)
Honda Gold Wing 1200 (USA)
(84 - 87)
Honda Gold Wing 1500 (USA)
(88 - 98)
Honda H100 & H100S Singles
(80 - 92)

Honda MB, MBX, MT & MTX50
(80 - 93)
Honda MBX/MTX125 & MTX200
(83 - 93)
Honda NB, ND, NP & NS50 Melody
(81 - 85)
Honda NE/NB50 Vision & SA50 Vision
Met-in (85 - 95)
Honda NS125 (86 - 93)
Honda NTV600 & 650 V-Twins
(88 - 96)
Honda Prelude CVCC (79 - 89)
Honda Shadow VT1100 (USA)
(85 - 98)
Honda Shadow VT600 & 750 (USA)
(88 - 99)
Honda ST1100 Pan European V-Fours
(90 - 97)
Honda TRX300 Shaft Drive ATVs
(88 - 95)
Honda TRX300EX & TRX400EX
ATVs (93 - 99)
Honda V45/65 Sabre & Magna
(82 - 88)
Honda VFR400 (NC30) & RVF400
(NC35) V-Fours (89 - 98)
Honda VFR750 & 700 V-Fours
(86 - 97)
Honda XL/XR 250 & 500 (78 - 84)
Honda XL/XR 80, 100, 125, 185 &
200 2-valve Models (78 - 87)
Honda XL600R & XR600R
(83 - 96)
Honda XR250L, XR250R & XR400R
(86 - 97)
Honda XR80R & XR100R (85 - 96)
Honda's V-Force *Julian Ryder*
Hyundai Excel (86 - 94)
Hyundai Pony (85 - 94) C to M
In-Car Entertainment Manual
(3rd Edition) *Dave Pollard*
Isuzu Rodeo & Honda Passport
(91 - 97)
Isuzu Trooper & Pick-up (81 - 93)
It Beats Working *Eoin Young*
Jackie Stewart *Karl Ludvigsen*
Jacques Villeneuve (2nd Edition)
Christopher Hilton
Jaguar E Type (61 - 72) up to L
Jaguar E-Type: The definitive history
Philip Porter
Jaguar Mk I & II, 240 & 340 (55 - 69)
up to H

Jaguar XJ12, XJS & Sovereign; Daimler Double Six (72 - 88) up to F

Jaguar XJ6 & Sovereign (Oct 86 - Sept 94) D to M

Jaguar XJ6 Purchase and Restoration Guide *Dave Pollard*

Jaguar XJ6, XJ & Sovereign; Daimler Sovereign (68 - Oct 86) up to D

Jaguar XK Engine *Dave Pollard*

Jaguar: Haynes Classic Makes Series *Martin Buckley*

Jaguar: The complete illustrated history (3rd Edition) *Philip Porter*

Jeep Cherokee Petrol (93 - 96) K to N

Jeep CJ (49 - 86)

Jeep Grand Cherokee (93 - 98)

Jeep Wagoneer & Pick-up (72 - 91)

Jeep Wranglar (87 - 95)

Jim Clark *Eric Dymock*

Jordan: Formula 1 racing team *David Tremayne*

Juan Manuel Fangio *Karl Ludvigsen*

Kawasaki 250, 350 & 400 Triples (72 - 79)

Kawasaki 400 & 440 Twins (74 - 81)

Kawasaki 400, 500 & 550 Fours (79 - 91)

Kawasaki 650 Four (76 - 78)

Kawasaki 750 Air-cooled Fours (80 - 91)

Kawasaki 900 & 1000 Fours (73 - 77)

Kawasaki AE/AR 50 & 80 (81 - 95)

Kawasaki EN450 & 500 Twins (Ltd/Vulcan) (85 - 93)

Kawasaki EX & ER500 (GPZ500S & ER-5) Twins (87 - 99)

Kawasaki KC, KE & KH100 (75 - 99)

Kawasaki KMX125 & 200 (86 - 96)

Kawasaki ZR550 & 750 Zephyr Fours (90 - 97)

Kawasaki ZX600 (GPZ600R, GPX600R, Ninja 600R & RX) & ZX750 (GPX750R, Ninja 750R) Fours (85 - 97)

Kawasaki ZX600 (Ninja ZX-6, ZZ-R600) Fours (90 - 97)

Kawasaki ZX-6R Ninja Fours (95 - 98)

Kawasaki ZX750 (Ninja ZX-7 & ZXR750) Fours (89 - 96)

Kawasaki ZX900, 1000 & 1100 Liquid-cooled Fours (83 - 97)

Lada 1200, 1300, 1500 & 1600 (74 - 91) up to J

Lada Samara (87 - 91) D to J

Lambretta Innocenti *Nigel Cox*

Land Rover 90, 110 & Defender Diesel (83 - 95) up to N

Land Rover 90, 110 and Defender Restoration Manual *Lindsay Porter*

Land Rover Discovery Diesel (89 - 95) G to N

Land Rover Series I, II & III Restoration Manual *Lindsay Porter*

Land Rover Series II, IIA & III Petrol (58 - 85) up to C

Land Rover Series IIA & III Diesel (58 - 85) up to C

Land Rover: Simply the best *Martin Hodder*

Last of the Lightnings, The *Ian Black*

Lincoln Rear-wheel drive (70 - 96)

London Cycle Guide, The *Nicky Crowther*

Longbow *Robert Hardy*

Managing a Legend *Robert Edwards*

Mazda 323 & Protegé (90 - 97)

Mazda 323 (Mar 81 - Oct 89) up to G

Mazda 323 (Oct 89 - 98) G to R

Mazda 626 & MX-6 & Ford Probe (93 - 98)

Mazda 626 (May 83 - Sept 87) up to E

Mazda 626 (RWD) (79 - 82)

Mazda 626 and MX-6 (FWD) (83 - 91)

Mazda B-1600, B-1800 & B-2000 Pick-up (72 - 88) up to F

Mazda GLC (FWD) (81 - 85)

Mazda GLC (RWD) (77 - 83)

Mazda MPV (89 - 94)

Mazda MX-5 Miata (90 - 97)

Mazda Pick-ups (72 - 93)

Mazda RX-7 Rotary (79 - 85)

Mazda RX-7 Rotary (86 - 91)

McLaren: Formula 1 racing team *Alan Henry*

McLaren: The epic years *Alan Henry*

Mercedes-Benz 124 Series (85 - Aug 93) C to K

Mercedes-Benz 190 (84 - 88)

Mercedes-Benz 190, 190E & 190D Petrol & Diesel (83 - 93) A to L

Mercedes-Benz 200, 240, 300 Diesel (Oct 76 - 85) up to C

Mercedes-Benz 250 & 280 (123 Series) (Oct 76 - 84) up to B

Mercedes-Benz 250 & 280 (68 - 72) up to L

Mercedes-Benz 280, 123 Series (77 - 81)

Mercedes-Benz 350 & 450 (71 - 80)

Mercedes-Benz Diesel 123 Series (76 - 85)

Mercury Villager & Nissan Quest (93 - 98)

MG Collection, The: The Post-War Models *Richard Monk*

MG Collection, The: The Pre-War Models *Richard Monk*

MG Midget & AH Sprite (58 - 80) up to W

MG Midget & Austin-Healey Sprite Restoration Manual (2nd Edition) *Lindsay Porter*

MG: Haynes Classic Makes Series *Malcolm Green*

MGB (62 - 80) up to W

MGB Restoration Manual (2nd Edition) *Lindsay Porter*

MGB: The Illustrated History (2nd Edition) *Jonathan Wood & Lionel Burrell*

Mick Doohan *Mat Oxley*

Mighty Minis (3rd Edition) *Chris Harvey*

Mika Hakkinen *Christopher Hilton*

Military Aviation Disasters *David Gero*

Mini (59 - 69) up to H

Mini (69 - Oct 96) up to P

Mini Restoration Manual (2nd Edition) *Lindsay Porter*

Mitsubishi Cordia, Tredia, Galant, Precis & Mirage (83 - 93)

Mitsubishi Eclipse, Plymouth Laser & Eagle Talon (90 - 94)

Mitsubishi Pick-up & Montero (83 - 96)

Mitsubishi Shogun & L200 Pick-Ups (83 - 94) up to M

Model Railway Design Manual, The *C. J. Freezer*

Model Railway Manual, The *C. J. Freezer*

Modern Engine Tuning *A. Graham Bell*

Morgan: The Last Survivor *Chris Harvey*

Morris Ital 1.3 (80 - 84) up to B

Morris Minor & 1000 Purchase and

Restoration Guide *Lindsay Porter*
Morris Minor 1000 (56 - 71) up to K
Morris Minor *Jon Pressnell*
Moto Guzzi 750, 850 & 1000 V-Twins
   (74 - 78)
Moto Guzzi Story, The *Ian Falloon*
Motor Cycle Restorer's Workshop
   Companion *Geoff Purnell*
Motorcaravan Manual, The
   John Wickersham
Motorcycle Basics Manual
Motorcycle Electrical TechBook
   (3rd Edition)
Motorcycle Workshop Practice
   TechBook (2nd Edition)
Motorcyclists Welcome: The Peter
   Gleave Guide *Peter Gleave*
Mountain Biking *Dan Hope*
My First Bike Book *Frank Dickens*
MZ ETZ Models (81 - 95)
Napier: The first to wear the green
   David Venables
Naval Wargaming *Paul Hague*
Nissan 300ZX Turbo & non-Turbo
   models (84 - 89)
Nissan Altima (93 - 97)
Nissan Bluebird (Mar 86 - 90)
   C to H
Nissan Bluebird (May 84 - Mar 86)
   A to C
Nissan Cherry (Sept 82 - 86) up to D
Nissan Maxima (85 - 89)
Nissan Micra (83 - Jan 93) up to K
Nissan Micra (93 - 99) K to T
Nissan Pulsar (83 - 86)
Nissan Sentra & 200SX (95 - 98)
Nissan Sentra (82 - 94)
Nissan Stanza (82 - 86) up to D
Nissan Stanza (82 - 90)
Nissan Sunny (Apr 91 - 95) H to N
Nissan Sunny (May 82 - Oct 86)
   up to D
Nissan Sunny (Oct 86 - Mar 91)
   D to H
Nissan/Datsun Pick-ups & Pathfinder
   (80 - 96)
Norton 500, 600, 650 & 750 Twins
   (57 - 70)
Norton Commando (68 - 77)
Norton Motor Cycles from
   1950 to 1986 *Steve Wilson*
Off-Road 4-Wheel-Drive Book, The
   (4th Edition) *Jack Jackson*

Ogri Collection, The *Paul Sample*
Oldsmobile Cutlass (74 - 88)
Opel Ascona & Manta (B Series)
   (Sept 75 - 88) up to F
Opel Ascona (81 - 88)
Opel Astra (Oct 91 - Feb 98)
Opel Calibra (90 - 98)
Opel Corsa (83 - Mar 93)
Opel Corsa (Mar 93 - 97)
Opel Frontera Petrol & Diesel
   (91 - 98)
Opel Kadett (Nov 79 - Oct 84)
Opel Kadett (Oct 84 - Oct 91)
Opel Omega & Senator (86 - 94)
Opel Omega (94 - 99)
Opel Rekord (Feb 78 - Oct 86) up to D
Opel Vectra (Oct 88 - Oct 95)
Opel Vectra Petrol & Diesel (95 - 98)
Paint Finishes and Effects
   Peter & Paula Knott
Painting Your Home: Exterior
   Julian Cassell & Peter Parham
Painting Your Home: Interiors
   Julian Cassell & Peter Parham
Peugeot 1.7/1.8 & 1.9 litre Diesel
   Engine (82 - 96) up to N
Peugeot 106 Petrol & Diesel (91 - 98)
   J to S
Peugeot 2.0, 2.1, 2.3 & 2.5 litre Diesel
   Engines (74 - 90) up to H
Peugeot 205 (83 - 95) A to N
Peugeot 305 (78 - 89) up to G
Peugeot 306 Petrol & Diesel (93 - 99)
   K to T
Peugeot 309 (86 - 93) C to K
Peugeot 405 Diesel (88 - 96) E to N
Peugeot 405 Petrol (88 - 96) E to N
Peugeot 406 Petrol & Diesel (96 - 97)
   N to R
Peugeot 505 (79 - 89) up to G
Piaggio (Vespa) Scooters (91 - 98)
Polaris ATVs (85 to 97)
Pontiac Fiero (84 - 88)
Pontiac Firebird (70 - 81)
Pontiac Firebird (82 - 92)
Pontiac Mid-size Models (70 - 87)
Porsche 911 (65 - 85) up to C
Porsche 911 Restoration Manual
   Lindsay Porter & Peter Morgan
Porsche 911 Story (6th Edition)
   Paul Frère
Porsche 911: The Evolution
   Clauspeter Becker

Porsche 914 (4-cyl) (69 - 76)
Porsche 917 *Peter Morgan*
Porsche 924 & 924 Turbo (76 - 85)
   up to C
Porsche 924/944 Book, The
   Peter Morgan
Porsche 944 (83 - 89)
Proton (89 - 97) F to P
Race and Rally Car Source Book
   (4th Edition) *Allan Staniforth*
Race Without End *Maurice Hamilton*
RAF Bomber Stories
   Martin W. Bowman
Railway Modelling (8th Edition)
   Norman Simmons
Rally Navigation *Martin Holmes*
Range Rover Restoration Manual
   Dave Pollard
Range Rover V8 (70 - Oct 92)
   up to K
Rebuilding and Tuning Ford's Kent
   Crossflow Engine
   Peter & Valerie Wallage
Reich Intruders, The
   Martin W. Bowman
Reliant Robin & Kitten (73 - 83)
   up to A
Renault 18 (79 - 86) up to D
Renault 19 Diesel (89 - 95) F to N
Renault 19 Petrol (89 - 94) F to M
Renault 21 (86 - 94) C to M
Renault 25 (84 - 92) B to K
Renault 5 (Feb 85 - 96) B to N
Renault 9 & 11 (82 - 89) up to F
Renault Clio Diesel (91 - June 96)
   H to N
Renault Clio Petrol (91 - May 98)
   H to R
Renault Espace Petrol & Diesel
   (85 - 96) C to N
Renault File, The *Eric Dymock*
Renault Fuego (80 - 86) up to C
Renault Laguna Petrol & Diesel
   (94 - 96) L to P
Renault Mégane & Scénic Petrol &
   Diesel (96 - 98) N to R
Restoration of Vintage and
   Thoroughbred Motorcycles, The
   (2nd Edition) *Jeff Clew*
Reynard Story, The *Mike Lawrence*
Rochester Carburetor Manual
Rolls-Royce & Bentley: The history of
   the cars *Martin Bennett*

Rolls-Royce and Bentley: All models
from 1904 *Klaus-Josef Rossfeldt*
Rover 211, 214, 216, 218 & 220 Petrol
& Diesel (Dec 95 - 98) N to R
Rover 213 & 216 (84 - 89) A to G
Rover 214 & 414 (89 - 96) G to N
Rover 216 & 416 (89 - 96) G to N
Rover 3500 (76 - 87) up to E
Rover 414, 416 & 420 Petrol & Diesel
(May 95 - 98) M to R
Rover 618, 620 & 623 (93 - 97)
K to P
Rover 820, 825 & 827 (86 - 95)
D to N
Rover Metro, 111 & 114 (May 90 - 96)
G to N
Rover V8 Engine, The (2nd Edition)
David Hardcastle
Royal Air Force At War, The
Martin W. Bowman
Royal Yacht Britannia, The
(3rd Edition) *Brian Hoey*
Saab 90, 99 & 900 (79 - Oct 93)
up to L
Saab 900 (79 - 88)
Saab 900 (Oct 93 - 98) L to R
Saab 9000 (4-cyl) (85 - 95) C to N
Sailing Rigs & Spars
Matthew Sheahan
Saturn (91 - 99)
Seat Ibiza & Malaga (85 - 92) B to K
Senna, Ayrton: As time goes by
Christopher Hilton
Senna, Ayrton: His full car racing
record *Christopher Hilton*
Senna, Ayrton: The Legend Grows
Christopher Hilton
Skoda Estelle (77 - 89) up to G
Skoda Favorit (89 - 96) F to N
Skoda Felicia Petrol & Diesel (95 - 99)
M to T
Small Engine Repair Manual
Curt Choate & Robert Jex
Spreading My Wings
Diana Barnato Walker
Stencils and Stencilling
Paula & Peter Knott
Step-by-step Guide to Bedrooms and
Bathrooms, A *Heather Luke*
Step-by-step Guide to Cushions, A
Hilary More
Step-by-step Guide to Decorative
Details, A *Jenny Plucknett*

Stewart: Formula 1 racing team
David Tremayne
Stirling Moss *Stirling Moss with
Doug Nye*
Stirling Moss *Karl Ludvigsen*
Strong to Save
Ray and Susannah Kipling
SU Carburettors *A. K. Legg*
Subaru 1100, 1300, 1400 & 1600
(71 - 79)
Subaru 1600 & 1800 (80 - 94)
Subaru 1600 & 1800 (Nov 79 - 90)
up to H
Subaru Legacy (90 - 98)
Suspension, Steering and Driveline
Manual
Suzuki 100, 125, 185 & 250 Air-cooled
Trail bikes (79 - 89)
Suzuki GP100 & 125 Singles (78 - 93)
Suzuki GS/GSX1000, 1100 & 1150
4-valve Fours (79 - 88)
Suzuki GS/GSX250, 400 & 450 Twins
(79 - 85)
Suzuki GS/GSX550 4-valve Fours
(83 - 88)
Suzuki GS1000 Four (77 - 79)
Suzuki GS500E Twin (89 - 97)
Suzuki GS550 (77 - 82) & GS750
Fours (76 - 79)
Suzuki GS850 Fours (78 - 88)
Suzuki GSF600 & 1200 Bandit Fours
(95 - 97)
Suzuki GSX-R600 & 750 (96 - 99)
Suzuki GSX-R750, GSX-R1100
(85 - 92), GSX600F, GSX750F,
GSX1100F (Katana) Fours
(88 - 96)
Suzuki GT, ZR & TS50 (77 - 90)
Suzuki GT250X7, GT200X5 & SB200
Twins (78 - 83)
Suzuki Samurai/Sidekick & Geo
Tracker (86 - 96)
Suzuki SJ Series, Samurai & Vitara
(4-cyl) (82 - 97) up to P
Talbot Alpine, Solara, Minx & Rapier
(75 - 86) up to D
Talbot Horizon (78 - 86) up to D
Talbot Samba (82 - 86) up to D
Titanic Disaster, The *Dave Bryceson*
Titanic: A Journey Through Time
John P. Eaton & Charles A. Haas
Titanic: Destination Disaster
(2nd Edition)

John P. Eaton & Charles A. Haas
Titanic: Triumph and Tragedy
(2nd Edition)
John P. Eaton & Charles A. Haas
Titanic: Women and Children First
Judith B. Geller
Toyota Camry & Avalon (92 - 96)
Toyota Camry (83 - 91)
Toyota Camry (97 - 99)
Toyota Carina E (May 92 - 97) J to P
Toyota Celica Front-wheel drive
(86 - 93)
Toyota Celica Rear-wheel drive
(71 - 85)
Toyota Celica Supra (79 - 92)
Toyota Corolla & Geo Prizm (93 - 97)
Toyota Corolla (75 - 79)
Toyota Corolla (80 - 85) up to C
Toyota Corolla (Aug 92 - 97) K to P
Toyota Corolla (Sept 83 - Sept 87)
A to E
Toyota Corolla (Sept 87 - Aug 92)
E to K
Toyota Corolla Front-wheel drive
(84 - 92)
Toyota Corolla Rear-wheel drive
(80 - 87)
Toyota Corolla Tercel (80 - 82)
Toyota Corona (74 - 82)
Toyota Cressida (78 - 82)
Toyota Hi-Ace & Hi-Lux (69 - Oct 83)
up to A
Toyota Land Cruiser (68 - 82)
Toyota Land Cruiser (80 - 96)
Toyota MR2 (85 - 87)
Toyota Pick-up (79 - 95)
Toyota Previa (91 - 95)
Toyota Tacoma, 4Runner & T100
(93 - 98)
Toyota Tercel (87 - 94)
TR for Triumph *Chris Harvey*
Triumph 350 & 500 Unit Twins
(58 - 73)
Triumph 650 & 750 2-valve Unit Twins
(63 - 83)
Triumph Acclaim (81 - 84) up to B
Triumph GT6 & Vitesse (62 - 74)
up to N
Triumph Motor Cycles from 1950 to
1988 *Steve Wilson*
Triumph Pre-Unit Twins (47 - 62)
Triumph Spitfire (62 - 81) up to X
Triumph Stag (70 - 78) up to T

Triumph Tiger 100 and Daytona
J. R. Nelson
Triumph Tiger Cub & Terrier (52 - 68)
Triumph TR7 (75 - 82) up to Y
Triumph Trident & BSA Rocket 3
(69 - 75)
Triumph Triples & Fours (carburettor
engines) (91 - 99)
Tuning Rover V8 Engines
David Hardcastle
Tuning the A-Series Engine (3rd
Edition) *David Vizard*
Twice Lucky *Stuart Turner*
Two-Stroke Performance Tuning
(2nd Edition) *A. Graham Bell*
USAAF Fighter Stories *Ian McLachlan*
Vauxhall Astra & Belmont
(Oct 84 - Oct 91) B to J
Vauxhall Astra (80 - Oct 84) up to B
Vauxhall Astra (Oct 91 - Feb 98) J to R
Vauxhall Carlton & Senator
(Nov 86 - 94) D to L
Vauxhall Carlton (Oct 78 - Oct 86)
up to D
Vauxhall Cavalier (81 - Oct 88)
up to F
Vauxhall Cavalier (Oct 88 - 95) F to N
Vauxhall Cavalier 1600, 1900 & 2000
(75 - July 81) up to W
Vauxhall Chevette (75 - 84) up to B
Vauxhall Corsa (Mar 93 - 97) K to R
Vauxhall Nova (83 - 93) up to K
Vauxhall Vectra Petrol & Diesel
(95 - 98) N to R
Vauxhall/Opel 1.5, 1.6 & 1.7 litre
Diesel Engine (82 - 96) up to N
Vauxhall/Opel Calibra (90 - 98)
G to S
Vauxhall/Opel Frontera Petrol & Diesel
(91 - Sept 98) J to S
Vauxhall/Opel Omega (94 - 99) L to T
V-Bombers *Tim Laming*
Vespa P/PX125, 150 & 200 Scooters
(78 - 95)
Vespa Scooters (59 - 78)
Vespa: An Illustrated History
Eric Brockway
Vintage Motorcyclists' Workshop, The
Radco
Volkswagen Beetle & Karmann Ghia
(54 - 79)
Volkswagen Beetle 1200 (54 - 77)
up to S

Volkswagen Beetle 1300 & 1500
(65 - 75) up to P
Volkswagen Beetle 1302 & 1302S
(70 - 72) up to L
Volkswagen Beetle 1303, 1303S & GT
(72 - 75) up to P
Volkswagen Dasher (74 - 81)
Volkswagen Golf & Jetta (93 - 97)
Volkswagen Golf & Jetta Mk 1 1.1 &
1.3 (74 - 84) up to A
Volkswagen Golf & Jetta Mk 1 Diesel
(78 - 84) up to A
Volkswagen Golf & Jetta Mk 2
(Mar 84 - Feb 92) A to J
Volkswagen Golf & Vento Petrol &
Diesel (Feb 92 - 96) J to N
Volkswagen Golf, Jetta & Scirocco
Mk 1, 1.5, 1.6 & 1.8 (74 - 84)
up to A
Volkswagen LT vans & light trucks
(76 - 87) up to E
Volkswagen Passat & Santana
(Sept 81 - May 88) up to E
Volkswagen Passat Petrol & Diesel
(May 88 - 96) E to P
Volkswagen Polo & Derby (76 - Jan 82)
up to X
Volkswagen Polo (82 - Oct 90) up to H
Volkswagen Polo (Nov 90 - Aug 94)
H to L
Volkswagen Rabbit, Jetta, Scirocco,
Pick-up & Convertible (gasoline
engine) (75 - 92)
Volkswagen Scirocco (82 - 90) up to H
Volkswagen Transporter (air-cooled)
(79 - 82) up to Y
Volkswagen Transporter (water-cooled)
(82 - 90) up to H
Volkswagen Transporter 1600 (68 - 79)
up to V
Volkswagen Transporter 1700, 1800
& 2000 (72 - 79) up to V
Volkswagen Type 3 1500 & 1600
(63 - 73)
Volkswagen Vanagon air-cooled
(80 - 83)
Volvo 120 & 130 Series (61 - 73)
Volvo 142, 144 & 145 (66 - 74)
up to N
Volvo 240 Series (74 - 93) up to K
Volvo 240 Series (76 - 93)
Volvo 262, 264 & 260/265 (75 - 85)
up to C

Volvo 340, 343, 345 & 360 (76 - 91) up
to J
Volvo 440, 460 & 480 (87 - 97) D to P
Volvo 740 & 760 (82 - 91) up to J
Volvo 740 & 760 Series (82 - 88)
Volvo 850 (92 - 96) J to P
Volvo 940 (90 - 96) H to N
Volvo S40 & V40 (96 - 99) N to V
VW Beetle and Transporter Restoration
Manual *Lindsay Porter*
Walks Along the Thames Path
Leigh Hatts
Wall Tiling Book, The *Alex Portelli*
Wallpapering Book, The
Julian Cassell & Peter Parham
Wartime Disasters at Sea
David Williams
Washer Drier & Tumbledrier Manual
Graham Dixon
Washing Machine Manual
Graham Dixon
Wayne Rainey *Michael Scott*
Weber Carburettors (to 79)
A. K. Legg
Weber/Zenith Stromberg/
SU Carburetor Manual
Whatever Happened to the British
Motorcycle Industry?
Bert Hopwood
Williams: Formula 1 racing team
Alan Henry
Works Minis, The (2nd Edition)
Peter Browning
World Encyclopaedia of Aero Engines
(4th Edition) *Bill Gunston*
World Encyclopaedia of the Tank
Christopher Chant
World Superbikes *Julian Ryder*
World's Major Airlines, The
David Wragg
Yamaha 250 & 350 Twins (70 - 79)
Yamaha 650 Twins (70 - 83)
Yamaha DT50 & 80 Trail Bikes
(78 - 95)
Yamaha FJ, FZ, XJ & YX600 Radian
(84 - 92)
Yamaha FJ1100 & 1200 Fours
(84 - 96)
Yamaha FZR600, 750 & 1000 Fours
(87 - 96)
Yamaha RD & DT125LC (82 - 87)
Yamaha RD250 & 350LC Twins
(80 - 82)

Yamaha RD350 YPVS Twins (83 - 95)
Yamaha RD400 Twin (75 - 79)
Yamaha RS/RXS100 & 125 Singles
(74 - 95)
Yamaha T50 & 80 Townmate (83 - 95)
Yamaha TDM850, TRX850 & XTZ750
(89 - 99)
Yamaha TY50, 80, 125 & 175
(74 - 84)
Yamaha TZR125 (87 - 93) & DT125R
(88 - 95)
Yamaha Warrior and Banshee ATVs
(87 - 99)

Yamaha XJ600S (Diversion, Seca II)
& XJ600N Fours (92 - 99)
Yamaha XJ650 & 750 Fours (80 - 84)
Yamaha XJ900F Fours (83 - 94)
Yamaha XS250, 360 & 400 sohc Twins
(75 - 84)
Yamaha XS750 & 850 Triples (76 - 85)
Yamaha XT & SR125 (82 - 96)
Yamaha XT, TT & SR500 Singles
(75 - 83)
Yamaha XV V-Twins (81 - 96)
Yamaha XZ550 Vision V-Twins
(82 - 85)

Yamaha YB100 Singles (73 - 91)
Yamaha YFB250 Timberwolf ATV
(92 - 96)
Yamaha YFM350 Big Bear and ER
ATVs (87 - 95)
Yamaha YFS200 Blaster ATV (88 - 98)
Yamaha YT, YFM, YTM & YTZ ATVs
(80 - 85)
Yugo/Zastava (81 - 90) up to H

Foreign language titles

French

Guide de votre Caravane, Le
Ally Watson
Guide du Vélo de course, Le
Steve Thomas, Dave Smith
& Ben Searle
Audi 80, 90 et Coupé essence
(86 - 90)
BMW Séries 3 & 5 essence (82 - 93)
Citroën AX essence et Diesel (86 - 98)
Citroën BX essence (82 - 95)
Citroën BX Diesel (83 - 95)
Citroën Saxo essence et Diesel
(96 - 99)
Citroën Visa essence (79 - 88)
Citroën Xantia essence et Diesel
(93 - 98)
Citroën XM essence et Diesel
(89 - 98)
Citroën ZX essence (91 - 96)
Citroën ZX Diesel (91 - 96)
FIAT Panda essence (80 - 92)
FIAT Punto essence et Diesel (93 - 97)
FIAT Uno essence (83 - 95)
Ford Escort & Orion essence (80 - 90)
Ford Fiesta essence (Août 83 - Fév 89)
Ford Fiesta essence (89 - 95)
Ford Fiesta IV essence et Diesel
(Sept 95 - 99)
Ford Moteurs Diesel (84 - 96)
Mercedes-Benz 190 essence et Diesel
(82 - 94)
Opel Astra essence et Diesel (91 - 98)
Opel Corsa essence (83 - 93)
Opel Corsa essence et Diesel (93 - 98)
Opel Moteurs Diesel (82 - 96)

Opel Vectra essence et Diesel (95 - 98)
Peugeot 104 essence (73 - 88)
Peugeot 106 essence et Diesel
(91 - 99)
Peugeot 205 essence (83 - 98)
Peugeot 205 Diesel (83 - 98)
Peugeot 305 essence (77 - 91)
Peugeot 306 essence et Diesel
(93 - 99)
Peugeot 309 essence (85 - 96)
Peugeot 405 essence (87 - 96)
Peugeot 405 Diesel (88 - 98)
Peugeot 406 essence et Diesel
(95 - 97)
Renault 5 essence (72 - 85)
Renault Super 5 & Express essence
(84 - 96)
Renault Super 5 & Express Diesel
(85 - 95)
Renault 9 & 11 essence (81 - 89)
Renault 18 essence (78 - 86)
Renault 19 essence (88 - 97)
Renault 19 Diesel (88 - 97)
Renault 21 essence (86 - 94)
Renault 21 Diesel (86 - 96)
Renault 25 essence et Diesel
(84 - 94)
Renault Clio essence (90 - avril 96)
Renault Clio Diesel (90 - avril 96)
Renault Espace essence et Diesel
(84 - 96)
Renault Laguna essence et Diesel
(94 - 96)
Renault Mégane/Scénic essence et
Diesel (95 - 98)
Renault Twingo essence (93 - 96)

Volkswagen Golf II & Jetta essence
(84 - 92)
Volkswagen Golf III & Vento essence et
Diesel (92 - 99)
Volkswagen Passat III essence et Diesel
(88 - 96)
Volkswagen Polo essence (81 - 90)
Volkswagen Polo III essence et Diesel
(94 - 99)

Russian

Audi 80, 90 & Coupé (86 - 90)
Mercedes-Benz 200, 230, 250, 260,
280, 300 & 320 (85 - 93)
Opel Vectra (88 - 95)
Peugeot 405 (88 - 96)
Toyota Carina E (92 - 97)
Volvo 850 (92 - 96)
TechBook: РУКОВОДСТВО ПО
ЭЛЕКТРИЧЕСКОМУ
ОБОРУДОВАНИЮ АВТОМОБИЛЕЙ

South African

VW Citi Golf (83 - 97)

Swedish

Audi 100 & 200 (82 - 90)
Audi 100 & A6 (maj 91 - maj 97)
BMW 3- & 5-serier (81 - 91)
Chevrolet & GMC Van (68 - 95)
Ford Escort (80 - 90)
Ford Escort & Orion (90 - 97)
Ford Mondeo (93 - 96)
Ford Scorpio (85 - 94)
Ford Sierra (82 - 93)
Mercedes-Benz 124-serien (85 - 93)

Mercedes-Benz 190, 190E & 190D
  (83 - 93)
Opel Kadett (84 - 91)
Opel Omega & Senator (86 - 94)
Opel Vectra (88 - 95)
Saab 90, 99 & 900 (79 - 93)
Saab 900 (okt 93 - 98)
Saab 9000 (85 - 95)
Volkswagen Golf & Jetta Mk II
  (84 - 92)
Volkswagen Golf III/Vento (92 - 96)
Volkswagen Passat & Santana (81 - 88)
Volkswagen Passat (88 - 96)
Volkswagen Transporter (82 - 90)
Volvo 240, 242, 244 & 245 (74 - 93)
Volvo 340, 343, 345 & 360 (76 - 91)
Volvo 440, 460 & 480 (87 - 92)
Volvo 740, 745 & 760 (82 - 92)
Volvo 850 (92 - 96)

Volvo 940 (91 - 96)
Bilens elektriska och elektroniska
  system
Bilens felkodssystem: Handbok för
  avläsning och diagnostik
Bilens motorstyrning och
  bränsleinsprutningssystem
Dieselmotorn - servicehandbok

Spanish

Reparación de Carroceria & Pintura
Códigos Automotrices de la
  Computadora
Manual de Frenos Automotriz
Inyección de Combustible (86 - 94)
Chevrolet/GMC Camionetas (67 - 91)
Chevrolet/GMC Camionetas (88 - 95)
Chevrolet/GMC Camionetas Cerradas
  (68 - 95)

Dodge Caravan, Plymouth Voyager,
  Chrysler Town & Country (84 - 95)
Ford Camionetas & Bronco (80 - 94)
Ford Camionetas Cerradas (69 - 91)
Ford & Mercury Modelos de Tamaño
  Grande (75 - 87)
Ford & Mercury Modelos de Tamaño
  Mediano (75 - 86)
Ford Taurus & Mercury Sable (86 - 95)
General Motors Modelos de Tamaño
  Grande (70 - 90)
General Motors Modelos de Tamaño
  Mediano (70 - 88)
Nissan/Datsun Camionetas &
  Pathfinder (80 - 96)
Nissan Sentra (82 - 94)
Toyota Camionetas & 4-Runner
  (79 - 95)

Index